PATCHWORK PICTURES

 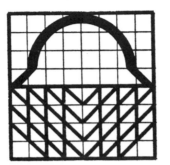  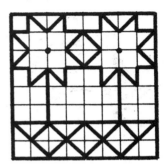

PATCHWORK PICTURES

1001 PATTERNS FOR PIECING

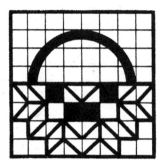

Carol LaBranche

Patterns Rendered by Donald Rolfe

THE MAIN STREET PRESS • PITTSTOWN, NEW JERSEY

This book is dedicated to my mother, who never made a quilt but always kept me warm in many, many other ways.

First edition 1985

All rights reserved
Copyright © 1985 by Carol LaBranche

Published by
The Main Street Press, Inc.
William Case House
Pittstown, NJ 08867

Published simultaneously in Canada by
Methuen Publications
2330 Midland Avenue
Agincourt, Ontario M1S 1P7

Printed in the United States of America

Library of Congress Cataloging in Publication Data

LaBranche, Carol.
  Patchwork pictures.

  Bibliography: p. 126
  1. Quilting. 2. Patchwork. I. Title.
TT835.L26 1985   746.9'7   85-4988
ISBN 0-915590-70-0
ISBN 0-915590-69-7 (pbk.)

Contents

Preface

THIS book came into being because I never know when to stop. I started out to make a simple pieced house quilt and got carried away collecting patterns. I couldn't seem to make up my mind which of the many house patterns I wanted to use. The more I looked through quilt collections, the more patterns I found—salt boxes, log cabins, mansions, and more modest dwellings. My imagined quilt got more complex as I discovered patterns for trees and flowers to go around my house, airplanes to fly over it, and hearts to show my affection for it. Soon I had sheets of graph-paper designs and a treasure hunt in progress. My quilt got lost in the future as the search continued for more patterns that represented real things.

Most pieced patterns are purely abstract, even if they have names like Rocky Road, Broken Dishes, or Ocean Wave. They may suggest these things, but they do not actually illustrate or represent them. When early quilters wanted to make a recognizable image of something—a flower, a person, a horse—they usually resorted to appliqué, which is amenable to any shape the experienced stitcher can stitch around. Poor stitchers wind up with lumps instead of flowers. Piecing is more forgiving but also more geometric. Curved lines exist in patchwork, but are always more difficult to achieve. Simple shapes made of straight lines are the natural order of piecing. However, this does not rule out certain kinds of images. In my travels through the quilt world, I discovered lots of houses, trees, flowers, and baskets. In traditional quilts I also found alphabets, praising the Lord or teaching a child to read. And occasionally I'd find an odd fellow—a butterfly, a bird, a train, a cat. The pile of graph paper grew.

At last I'd exhausted the traditional quilt pattern sources, but by that time I'd begun to think of other kinds of simple pictorial patterns. Various textile crafts use graph patterns, notably jacquard woven coverlets, needlepoint and cross-stitch, intarsia knitting and crochet. Many of these patterns can be translated easily into quilting patterns, and so they have been in the pages that follow. I also have included a few ideas of my own, notably the broken hearts. Other pictorial pieced patterns are still waiting to be discovered or invented. I'd like to see more flowers, animals, and household objects, as well as more twentieth-century images. There are lots of Little Red Schoolhouses, for example, but I had to invent a skyscraper.

While on my search for picture patterns, I found I had to establish a few rules or go mad with indecision. Patterns that depend on special color schemes to give the appearance of an image were discarded as not being truly representational. Moon over the Mountain, for instance, is a triangle and a circle without the appropriate colors. Fans were left out as they are simply semicircles, just as Dresden Plate is a scalloped circle. Stars were a problem, as they are, in a sense, representational. I quickly realized, however, that there are so many of them that they deserve a book of their own, so they are not included here. I also tried to keep everything based on the grid, to make for easy template making, but I wasn't terribly rigid about enforcing this rule. Some appliquéd leaves and stems appear with the traditional pieced flowers, and some curved piecing lines are traditional and unavoidable.

The next step was to organize the patterns into something resembling common sense. What patterns went with what other patterns, and why? There are, for instance, many Trees of Paradise, and not all of them are even similar. And, vice versa, sometimes the same pattern has several names. Since the names added to the confusion rather than helping solve it, I left them out. Instead, the visual similarities between patterns decided what patterns went on what page and what order the pages were in. All of the one-story houses are grouped together, followed by the two-story houses. The headline on each page indicates the nature of the grouping. Each chapter is a separate entity, with its own internal organization dependent on its particular subject matter. The introduction to each chapter indicates its plan, tells how the patterns have been used in the past, and suggests some interpretations for contemporary quilts. In addition, patterns that seem related are cross-referenced. The hearts suggest flowers, the smoke in the train stacks works equally as well in the house chimneys.

It is my immodest hope that this collection will encourage quilters to bring a new kind of quilt into existence. As much as I like the dazzling displays of color and craftsmanship that are most contemporary quilts, and I do, they are often only artistic exercises. Color, shape, and line are artists' tools. Used as subject matter alone, they create feasts for the eye but leave the heart untouched. The patterns in this collection give the quilter something new to work with. They represent things in the world, things we know and care about. They are real subject matter. With them, pictures can be made, stories told, an emotion depicted, a message spoken. I would like to see new quilts that are deeply personal, that use subject matter to indicate values and feelings and desires.

The patterns in this collection are mostly simple, even occasionally naïve. Because they are simple, I hope they will be used boldly, freely, and with no concern other than personal expression. As I look through book after book on quilts, what strikes me is the great, even mad, freedom of the very best quilts. They are unembarrassed displays of strong personalities and strong emotions. They are quilts whose makers seem to sing their own individual song. So don't hold back; sing your song loud and clear and with feeling.

Introduction: Using Picture Patterns

THIS book is a collection of unique pieced patterns. The patterns are mostly simple ones, appropriate for a beginner, but this is not a how-to-make-a-quilt book. Lessons in a fabric store, or some help from a friend, or one of the books in the Bibliography (Beth Gutcheon's *The Perfect Patchwork Primer* is recommended) will be necessary to guide the first-time quilt maker. This section deals only with the mechanics of using these patterns and not with fabric selection, sewing machine techniques, or basic quilt construction.

DESIGN

Picture patterns can be used in several distinctly different manners. The traditional way is to repeat the same block. The visual effect, however, is different when the block has a recognizable image. The object that is represented takes on importance through repetition, while at the same time, paradoxically, it also becomes more a pattern and less a picture. Andy Warhol exploited this curious effect in the '60s with paintings that repeated images of Coke bottles and Campbell's Soup cans. The cup and saucer quilt (p. 112) has the same strange double nature. The coffeecup is significant, each one set apart, alone, immortalized in orderly rows. At the same time it is a simple shape and a common object. Through repetition it becomes more a pattern and less an image of a real object. More important, less important, all at the same time, and mysterious too. What are all those coffeecups doing there? Images always seem as though they have a message or a meaning, even if we aren't sure what it is.

Attention to scale in quilts of this kind of design is important. A quilt with lots of small coffeecups would have a different flavor than one with far fewer and/or much larger coffeecups. The number and the size of the images work together to produce varying kinds of messages.

Another way to use the picture patterns is to tilt them, or change their direction. If the pattern is repeated edge to edge, but at different angles, a secondary pattern is usually created. The airplane quilt (p. 111) and the well-known basket quilt that served as the model for the 1978 quilt stamp (see p. 80 for the setting) are examples of tilted or rearranged settings. The secondary pattern, always an abstract one, will create another paradoxical visual effect. Images always engage the eye, much more so than abstract patterns. People "see" images even where there are none, as in abstract paintings or the man in the moon. The desire is strong in all of us to see something recognizable. By changing the setting of the picture block from straight rows to tilted, the eye sees two things at the same time, the image and the secondary pattern. The latter will tend to deny the "reality" of the former. The eye (or the mind) likes having two very different things presented to it at the same time. It is a visual game to see two dissimilar kinds of things in the same work. If this kind of game is going to be used in designing a quilt, bigger scale blocks are probably better. Small blocks placed close together will tend to diminish the image and thus spoil the game. Both the image and the secondary pattern should be of the same visual weight.

Different picture patterns can also be combined in one quilt. There is no rule that says all baskets in one quilt must be exactly the same. "Variety is the spice of life," says the old cliché, which, like most clichés, is often true. Working with baskets, it is easy to make many different kinds of them into the same size block. It may be less easy to find a variety of flower blocks that can all be made the same size. If the chosen blocks do not differ greatly in size, some empty "space" can be added around the smaller blocks to bring them to the size of the largest block. For instance, if most of the blocks are 5 units by 5 units (on graph paper) but a few are 4 by 4, an extra unit can be added both horizontally and vertically, and, presto chango, all the blocks are 5 by 5. If this is not feasible, there is no rule that says all blocks in a quilt must be the same size. It will take a bit more figuring, and perhaps some additional fussing in the design process, but different size blocks can be fitted together into one quilt.

Another way to use these picture patterns is to blow one up to a huge size. The juggling clown quilt (p. 109) is one very large block. A giant sequoia or a generous heart might also make a striking quilt. Needless to say, these kinds of quilts go quite quickly. There are fewer pieces to cut and sew. Other quilts take the opposite approach and use tiny squares of fabric to build up a picture. These are called either "petit point" or "postage stamp" quilts because the detail is based on minute squares. The Little Home in Wyoming quilt (p. 35) is an example of this technique carried to great and wonderful extremes. A similar, simpler effect can be achieved by combining several patterns from this book and keeping the scale relatively small. Words and pictures also go well together, as witness the Jack and Jill quilt (p. 111).

Picture patterns can be combined to create thematic quilts. Think of all the ideas that say LOVE, translate them into images, and add an appropriate message in a pieced alphabet. Or a housework quilt (see p. 122 for appropriate subject matter) or a water quilt (lots of material for that) or a transportation quilt (boats, trains, airplanes, donkeys). There are lots of different themes that can be found in paging through these patterns.

Finally, consider making a complete picture—a townscape, your street, a garden. It may not be realistic in a photographic way, as pieced patterns are not perfectly naturalistic.

But all the ones contained in this book are easily recognizable as real objects. Combine them in a sensitive way and a picture will result.

The design possibilities are endless. To narrow down decision making, try a trick compliments of the Xerox machine. Make multiple copies of the patterns that are especially appealing or which relate to your theme. Cut out the individual graph-paper "blocks" from the Xerox paper and use them to "build" the quilt. For instance, make ten copies of the 5 by 5 page of baskets, cut out each basket block, and start moving the individual blocks around on an empty sheet of paper. You will find an arrangement that seems "right." Use the same trick to make a forest of trees, by Xeroxing all the upright trees, cutting them out, and arranging them according to size, smallest ones in the back to suggest perspective. The Xerox "blocks" are an easy way to pre-design a quilt. It is definitely easier than drawing out all the possibilities on graph paper. Make additional Xeroxes of the final design and use them for color studies. Felt-tip pens or colored pencils will give a rough idea of how the colors will work together, without having to buy and cut any fabric.

CONVERTING THE PATTERNS TO QUILT BLOCKS

Converting the graph-paper designs into full-size fabric blocks is less difficult than it sounds. It is a logical step-by-step activity. So, step by step:

1. The design is completed. You know how many different blocks you will be using, and what size each is to be. You therefore also know the finished size of your quilt.

2. Draw each block full size on graph paper. Tape two or more sheets together if necessary to give enough room for the entire block. To draw the block full size, count the number of graph-paper squares (units) high and wide the pattern takes. The sailboat below is 4 by 4 units square. Divide the number of units into the desired finished block size. If the

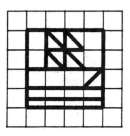

sailboat block is to be 8 inches square, each unit represents 2 inches. Measure 2 inch intervals on your graph paper and rule the horizontal and vertical lines. Using a straight edge, copy the picture pattern exactly on your 2 inch graph paper. You now have a full-scale drawing of the block.

Try to simplify your quiltmaking by making the size of the block easily divisible. There is less room for error if each unit is a round number. A unit of, say, 1⅝ inches is asking for trouble when it comes to measuring.

3. Analyze the design to determine the smallest number of pieces that have exactly the same size and shape. A separate template will be needed for each piece that has a different size and shape. The fewer pieces there are, the easier the quilt will be to cut and sew. In

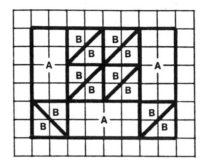

this sailboat there are only two different pieces, A and B. A is 2 units by 4 units. B is a triangle whose height and width comprise two units (but it is not an equilateral triangle). Only two templates will be needed, A and B.

This sailboat, however is more complicated.

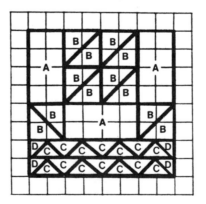

It contains four separate pieces and thus four templates will be necessary. A is the largest and D is the smallest. Analyzing each block takes practice, but it is not difficult. Try to keep the number of pieces low. Visualize how the block will be sewn together in the most efficient and easy way. In the sailboat above, all the B pieces should be sewn together first and then added to the A pieces. Next the C triangles are sewn together, adding the D pieces at each end. The CD strip is then sewn to the AB rectangle and the boat sails on the waves. Visualize the order of sewing, and the individual pieces of the same size and shape will become apparent.

4. Once the full-size block is drawn and the individual pieces determined, the last step is to make a template for each piece. Here I am going to suggest taking the easy way out. The marketplace today is full of pre-made templates of almost every size and shape. I've seen them for sale in heavy cardboard, acetate, heavyweight plastic, and metal. Take your full-size drawing to a quilt or fabric store and buy ready-made templates for each piece.

Nineteenth-century quilters bought tin templates whenever they could, so don't feel you are cheating by not making your own. Templates must be 100 percent accurate to be usable. The store-bought ones will be. The difficulties in drawing and cutting accurate templates are such that the manufactured ones are a small price to pay for accuracy. If your pattern pieces do not fit the existing templates or you simply want to do it yourself, I recommend Beth Gutcheon's book, or Judy Martin's *The Patchwork Book* (see Bibliography). Both give directions for making templates for both hand and machine sewing, regular and window ones.

5. Templates in hand, start cutting and then sewing!

1. Houses And Other Buildings

THE Little Red Schoolhouse is probably the most common representational patchwork quilt pattern. There are dozens of different versions, though most show a side view of a single-story house with a chimney. Few of the Schoolhouses have anything about them which actually suggests a school, such as a bell tower. It is a quilt mystery why the traditional name for the patterns that show a building should specify that it is a school when it looks more like a house. And if we associate schoolhouses with children, early quilters apparently did not. There are very few crib quilts with a Schoolhouse pattern, and other quilts with children's themes—toys and teddy bears, for example—are all twentieth-century.

Besides the stereotypical Schoolhouse, this section includes a variety of other kinds of houses—log cabins, salt boxes, Georgian mansions, and columned plantations. Early pattern makers did not worry about architectural exactness. Some of the houses would look very strange if one tried to build them. These are patterns, not renderings of real constructions.

The house patterns in this section have been categorized by building type, so all of the structures that have the same basic format are together. The houses seen frontally are separate from those with side views. One-story houses are separate from those with two. In addition, houses with exposed exterior chimneys, strong roof lines, and gables are separate from the rest. Some of the houses have homey details added, a picket fence, smoke coming out of the chimney, flowers, curtains or panes of glass in the windows. These are indicated rather randomly in some of the houses, but can be added to almost any of them. They call for additional piecing, perhaps some appliqué, embroidery, or special fabric choice. Let your building requirements and construction talents be your guide in deciding which, if any, to use.

After the houses come the other important buildings of nineteenth-century America—churches, barns, and train stations. Dutch windmills, common in some parts of the country, are also included. Because twentieth-century building types have been resolutely ignored by modern quilters, who seem to prefer the past, a skyscraper has been developed to add some hint of the modern world to contemporary quilts. An enterprising quilter/architect, armed with graph paper, could easily rebuild most cities. Modern buildings are based on repeating modules, just like quilts.

The simple boldness of the house patterns led few early quilters to experiment with them. The houses are usually lined up in stiff rows, and often made of red fabrics or scraps. Modern quilters need not stick to a single repeated pattern. Most blocks can be easily combined with stars, Delectable Mountains, trees, and flowers. Build your dream house, surrounded by other fantasies. The other sections of this book have lots of patterns for adding to your architectural dreams. There are also enough house blocks available to rebuild the average street, so don't stick to just one kind of house in your quilt. The house quilt has innumerable possibilities unexplored by fabric carpenters thus far.

One-Story Houses, SIDE VIEW

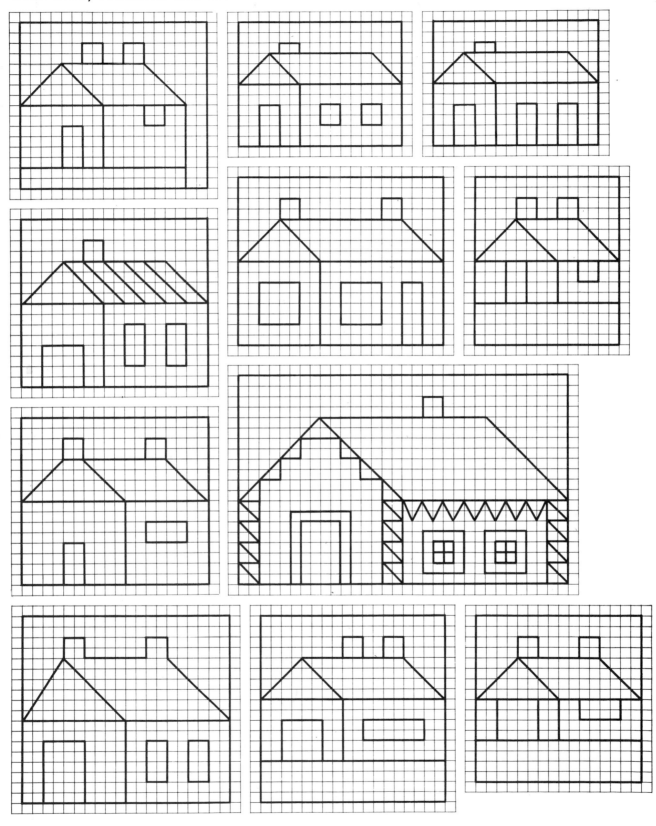

One-Story Houses, SIDE VIEW, CONTINUED

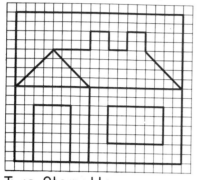

Two-Story Houses, SIDE VIEW

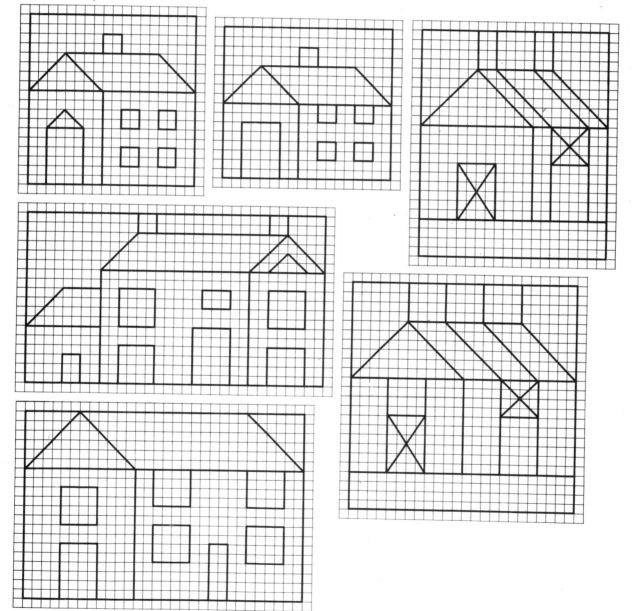

One- and Two-Story Houses, SIDE VIEW, STRONG ROOF LINE

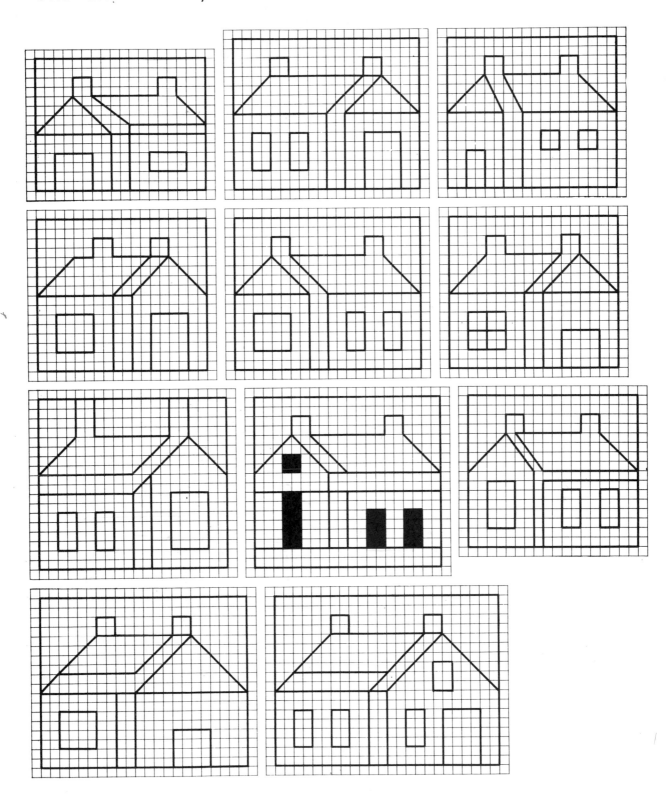

One- and Two-Story Houses, SIDE VIEW, STRONG ROOF LINE, CONTINUED

One-Story Houses, EXPOSED CHIMNEY

See color illustration, p. 36.

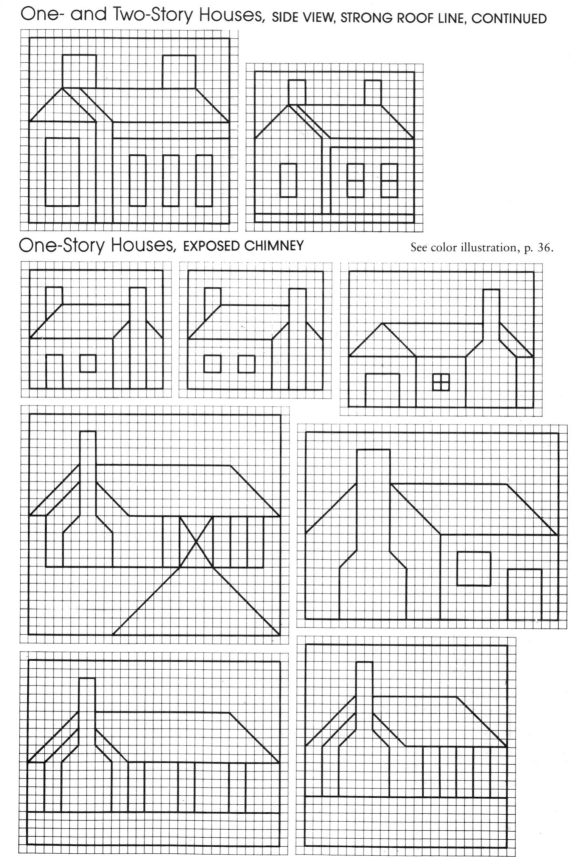

One-Story Houses, FRONT VIEW

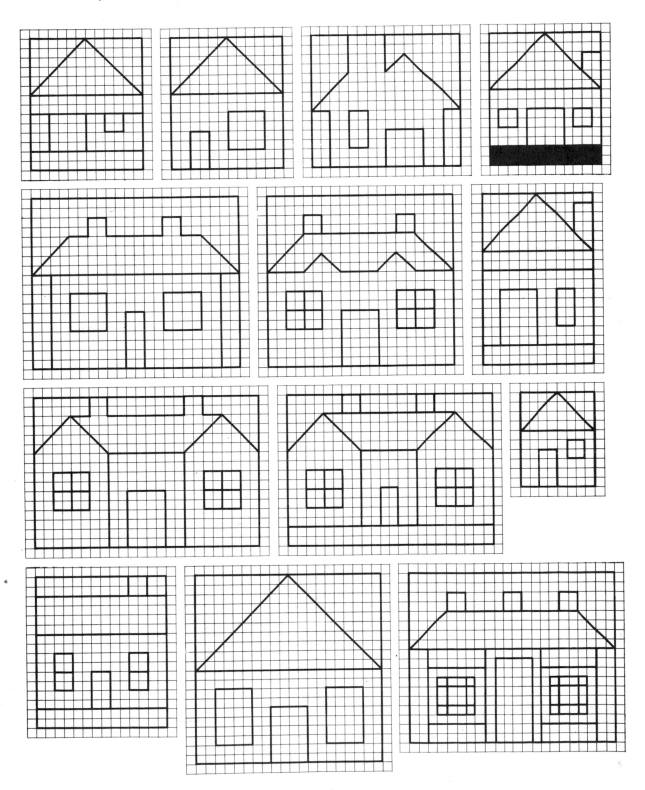

One-Story Houses, FRONT VIEW, CONTINUED

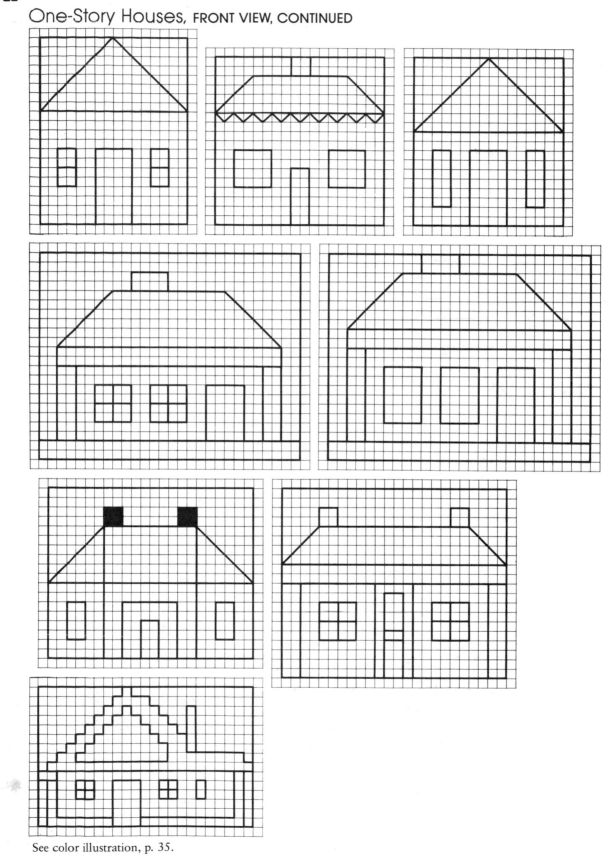

See color illustration, p. 35.

Two-Story Houses, FRONT VIEW

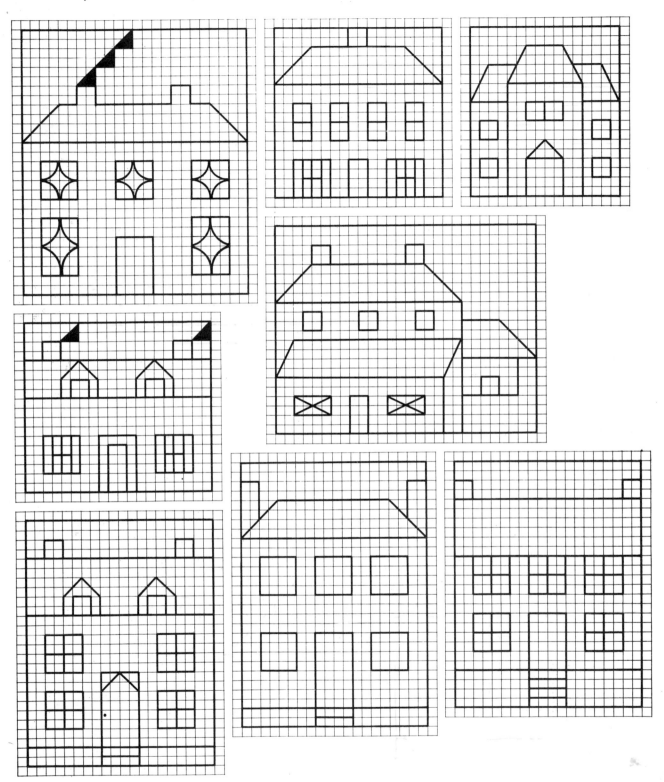

Two-Story Houses, FRONT VIEW, CONTINUED

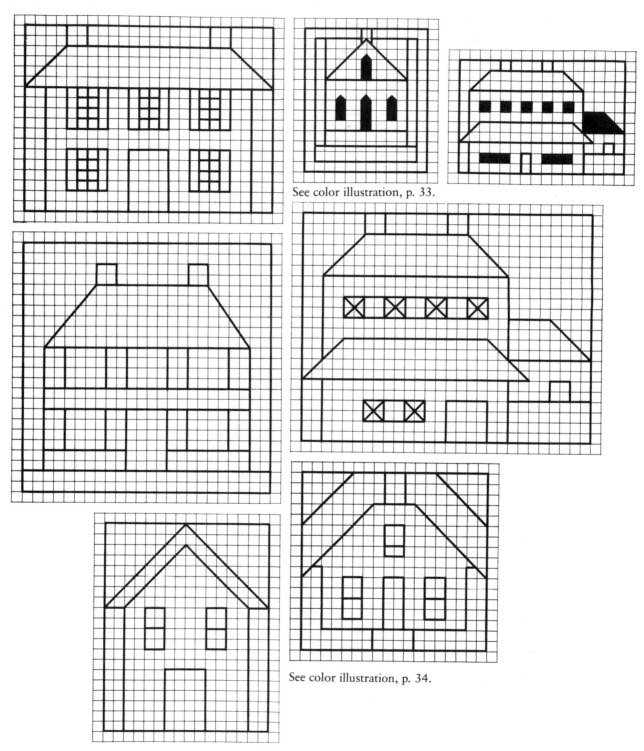

See color illustration, p. 33.

See color illustration, p. 34.

Two-Story Houses with Gable, FRONT VIEW

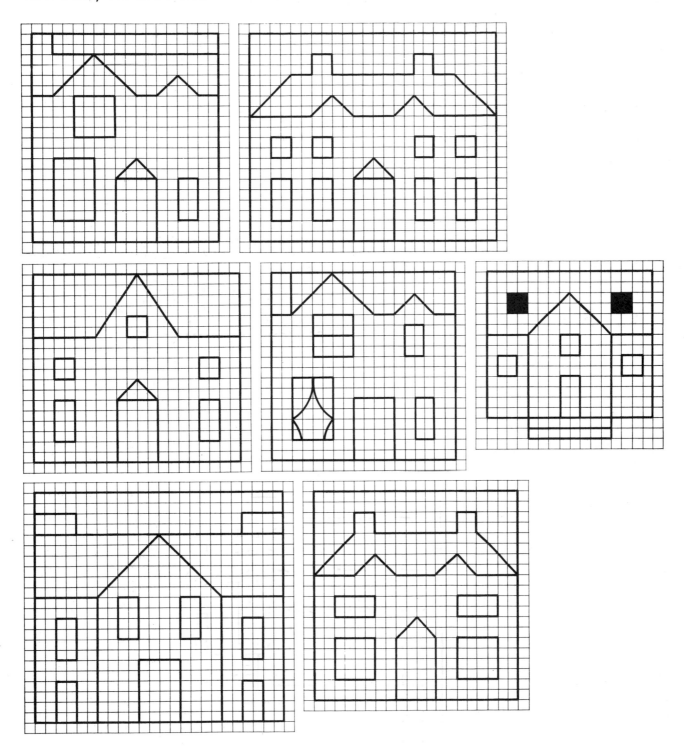

Two-Story Houses, MANSIONS

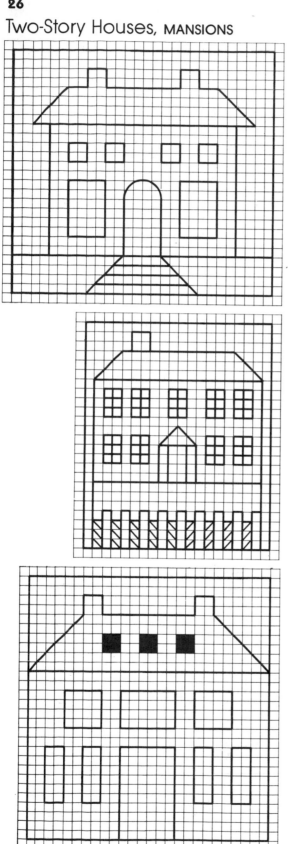

Salt Boxes

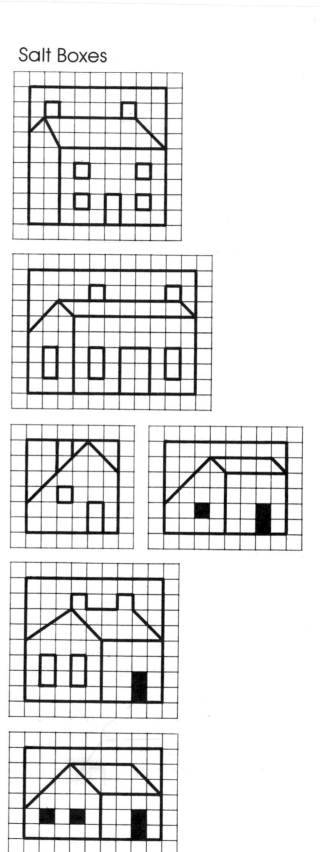

Log Cabins

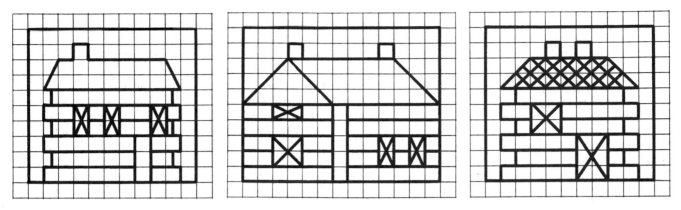

Log Cabin Piecing Houses

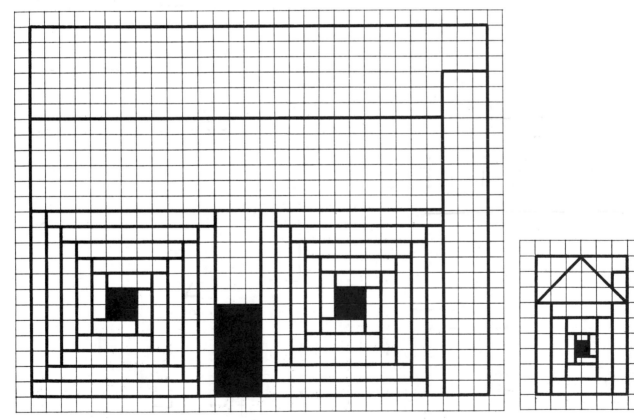

Churches

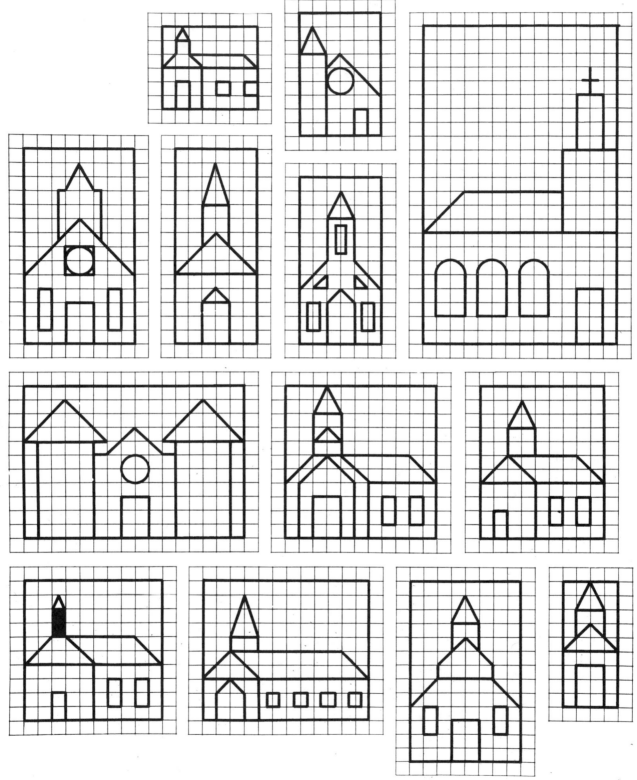

Churches, CONTINUED

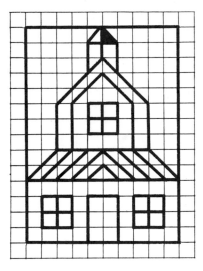 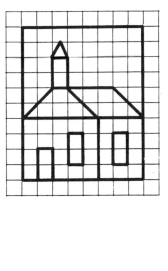 

Schoolhouses and Train Stations

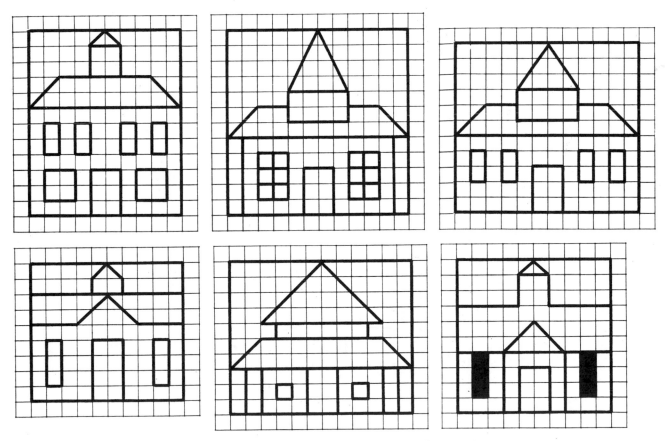

Barns

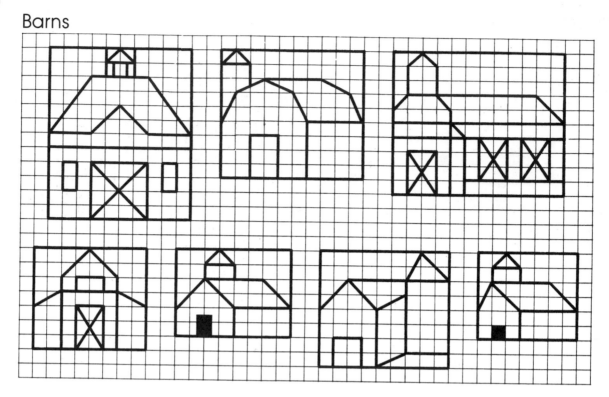

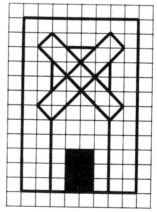

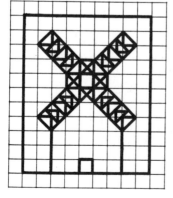

Windmills

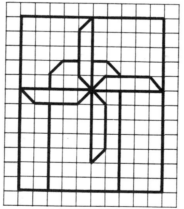

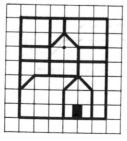

Miscellaneous

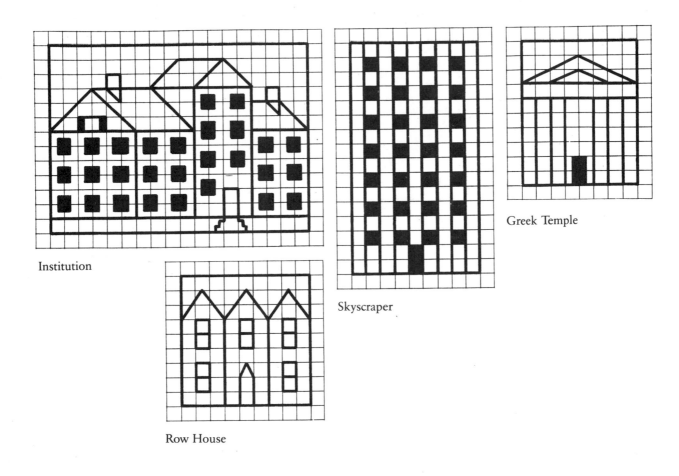

Institution

Skyscraper

Greek Temple

Row House

Architectural Details

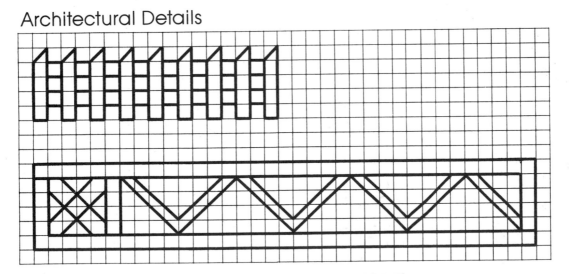

Fences

Architectural Details, CONTINUED

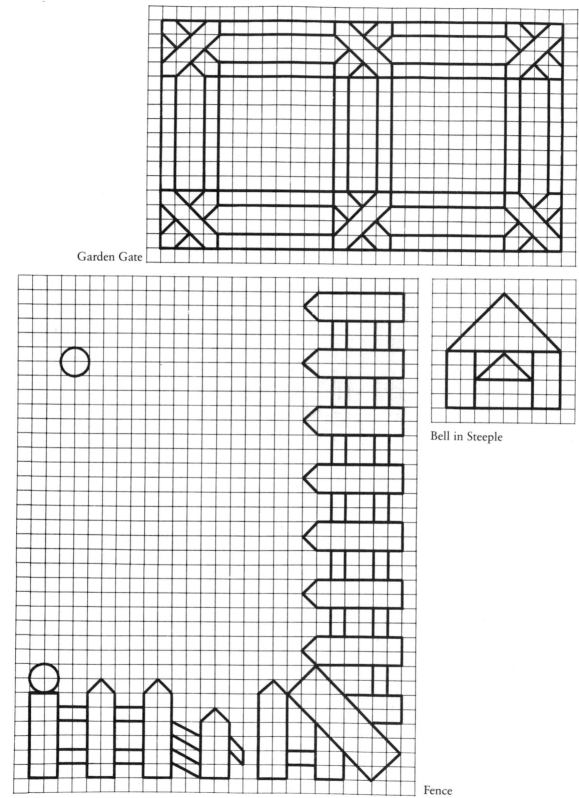

Garden Gate

Bell in Steeple

Fence

"Schoolhouse," New Hampshire, c. 1880, cotton, 77" x 76". See p. 24 for the black-and-white pieced front-view house design. Collection of Jonathan Holstein and Gail van der Hoof.

"Log House," New York State, c. 1890, wool. See p. 24 for an interpretation of the pieced house design. Collection of Susan Parrett and Rod Lich.

"Little Home in Wyoming," by Lillie L. Schenkel, Casper, Wyoming, 1936-37, cotton, 102″ x 88″. The quilt is composed of 12,457 pieces and is quilted along each one-inch square. See p. 22 for an interpretation of the pieced house design, and p. 57 for tree designs included in the quilt. Courtesy of Lillie L. Schenkel.

"Houses," Ohio, c. 1870, cotton, 80″ x 72″. See p. 20 for the repeating pieced house design. Collection of Phyllis Haders.

2. Flowers

FLOWERS are the most popular motif for appliquéd quilts, but they are not common in pieced work. Did the many forms of the Rose of Sharon, an appliquéd design, satisfy early quilters so that few pieced flower patterns were invented? Or did flowers just seem to demand the curves that come so naturally to appliqué and not to piecing? Pieced flowers, whatever their species, will always be patterns first—stylized, even stiff, usually formal. These characteristics were common to the Art Deco style of the '20s and '30s, and new flower patterns were created in that period. Ruby McKim's florid Oriental Poppy (p. 47) is a fine example, but it too has an appliquéd stem and leaf.

Because today's pattern designers seem to prefer realism in their flowers, they are forced to use complex curvilinear piecing and careful color shading. These kinds of flowers grow from fabric only with the greatest of care. They are hothouse beauties, one and all. The flowers in this section, however, are the simpler, traditional ones—the lily, the rose, the tulip. Naturalism is not their strength. A few look like a child's all-purpose generic "flower." They are clear two-dimensional patterns, easy to recognize and mostly simple to piece.

Flower blocks were traditionally set on the diagonal with a white block between them. Few early quilters thought of using the Garden Gate setting, though it would seem to be appropriate. (It is included in the first section on Houses, along with a variety of picket fences.) Fewer still mixed different kinds of flowers and thereby tried to "garden" with them. Real gardens always have more than one kind of flower in them, but quilts seldom do. It is, however, perfectly within the range of quilt possibility to combine different flowers in one quilt. Settings might be in the same manner as formal gardens, given the stylized nature of the plant material. Add birds, butterflies, paths (primrose or not), and trees to a garden—all are relevant, and patterns for them exist in other sections of this book. Real gardeners and quilt gardeners have much in common. Both harmonize color, size, and shape to create a pleasing design. But quilters need never worry about wilting, weeding, and watering.

Lilies

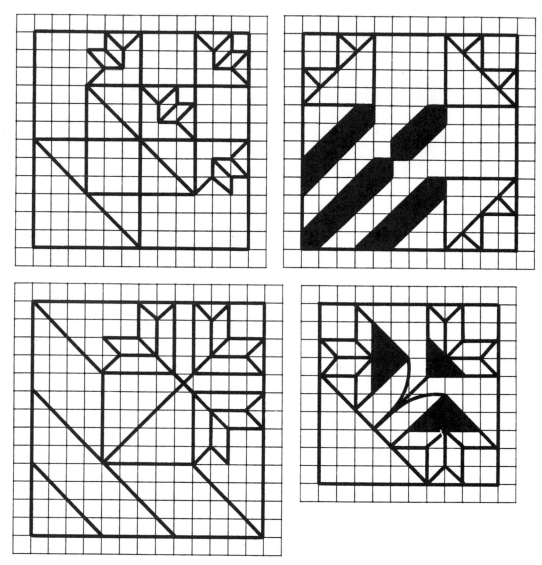

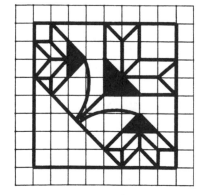

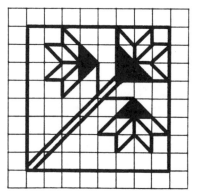

Appliqué stems are called for in many of the floral patterns. These are simple touches requiring only a minimum of time and effort.

Lilies, CONTINUED

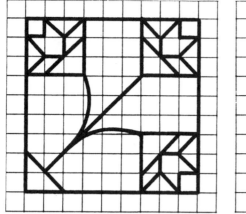
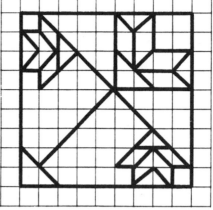

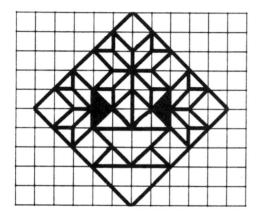
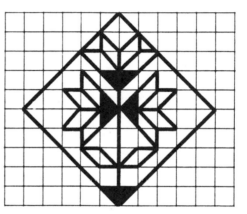

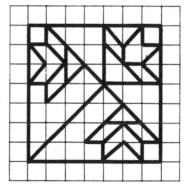

Roses

green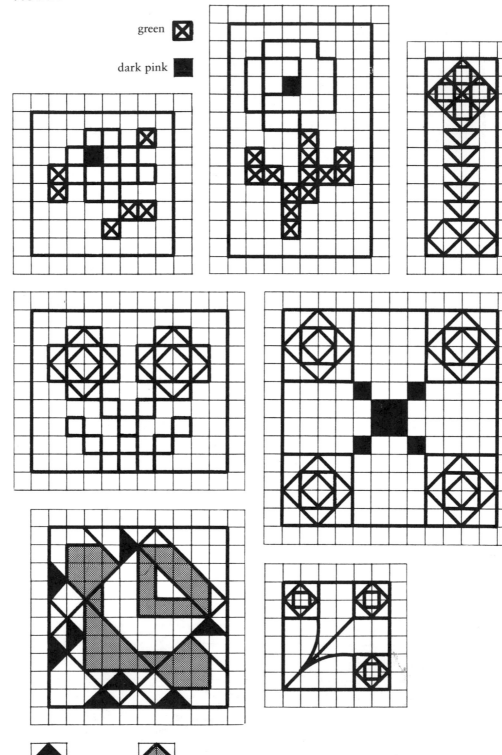

dark pink

green   dark pink

Sunflowers

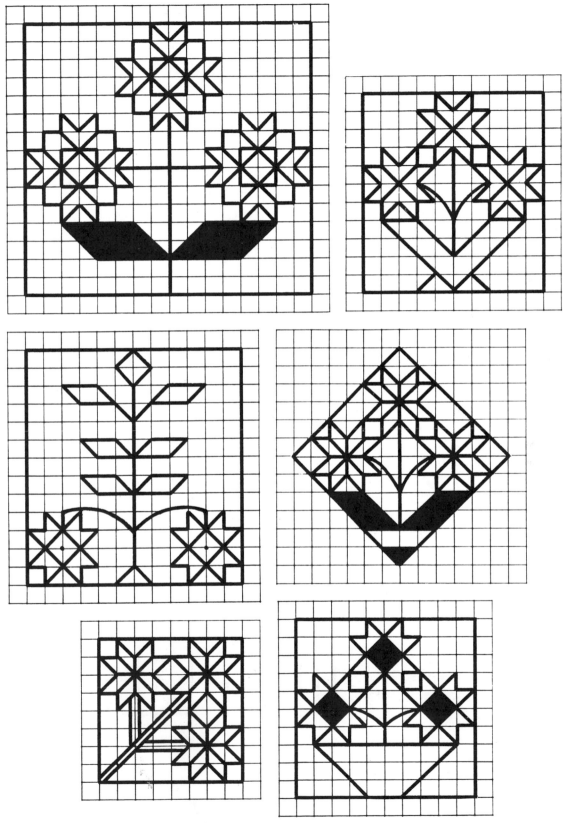

Tulips

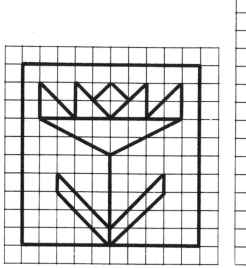
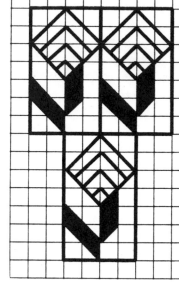
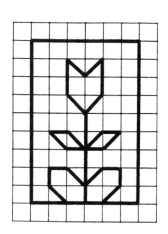

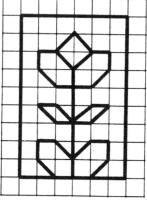
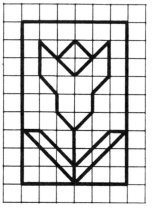

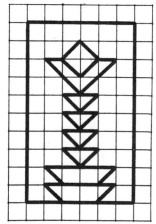
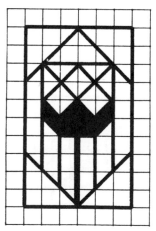
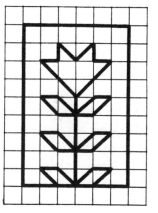

Tulips, CONTINUED

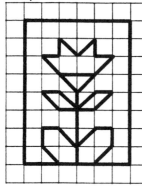  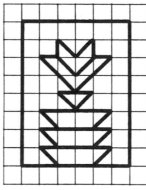 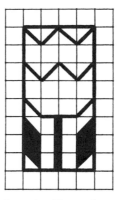

See color illustration, p. 53.

Miscellaneous Flowers

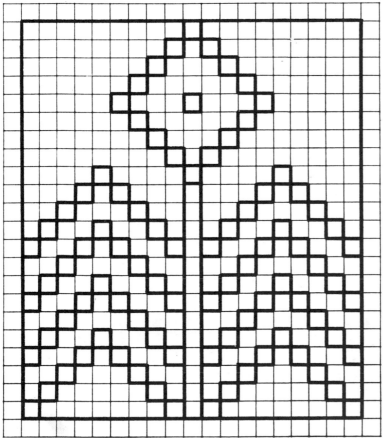 

Miscellaneous Flowers, CONTINUED

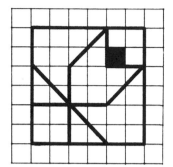

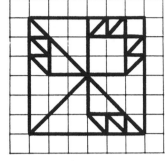

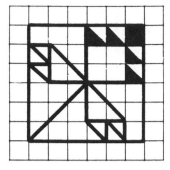

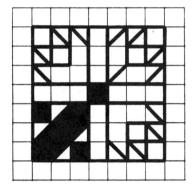

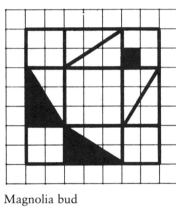

Magnolia bud

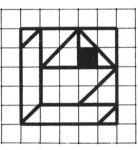

Magnolia bud

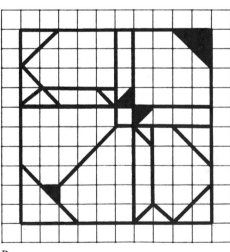

Pansy

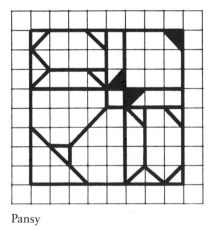

Pansy

Miscellaneous Flowers, CONTINUED

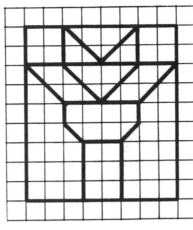

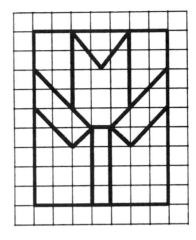

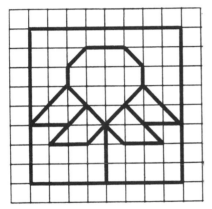

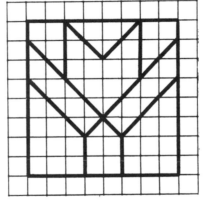

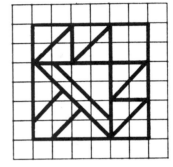

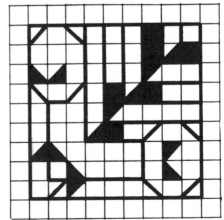

Trumpet Vine

Miscellaneous Flowers, CONTINUED

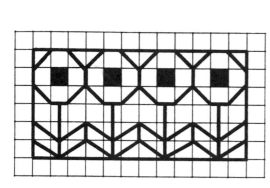

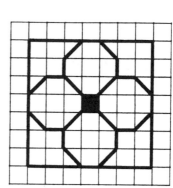

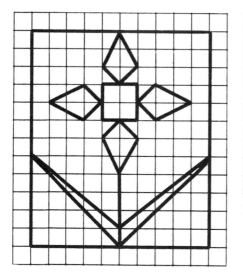

Each flower is made up of three Drunkard's Path patterns.

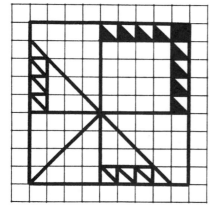

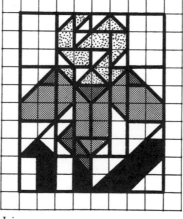

Iris

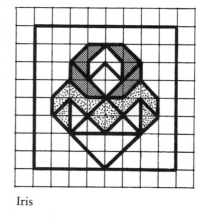

Iris

Miscellaneous Flowers, CONTINUED

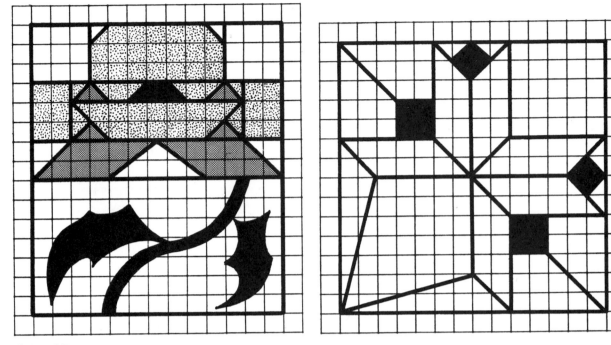

Oriental Poppy

3. Trees

TREES on quilts were popular with early settlers. They had a significance that was both real (trees were the raw material of much of daily life) and allegorical. The names given to tree patterns suggest some of their meanings—the Tree of Life, the Tree of Paradise, of Temptation, of Temperance, and Everlasting.

Tiny pieces of cloth were used for leaves, demanding careful piecing. The color scheme was generally green and white, with an occasional red or brown trunk. The trees stood straight and tall, often facing in two directions so that they could be seen as upright from either side of the bed. The effect was usually sober. This severity accounts perhaps for the fall from favor of the tree quilt in the exuberance of the late nineteenth century.

Trees suggest different things in the twentieth century. Temptation, Temperance, and Everlasting trees are images that now seem quaint rather than meaningful. Trees are no longer the raw material of life, as metal and plastic have usurped that role. Instead, trees are more often seen as the comfort and delight of the urbanized soul. They stand for strength and steadfastness, as they always have, but now also for beauty and pleasure. They are relief and refuge from contemporary plastic and metal. New kinds of tree quilts would seem to be needed to express the new ways we feel about trees and how we now use them.

The trees in this section are divided by design type. First are the leafy trees that stand diagonally in their block. Then diagonal trees with no apparent leaves. Next come trees that stand upright, first with leaves and then without. Then there is a collection of specialized trees—Christmas, flowering, and fruit. These need some attention to color so that the ornaments, flowers, apples, and cherries are distinguishable from the leaves. Finally, there are some very stylized trees adapted from coverlets, and a leaf collection. Other leaves can be found masquerading as flowers in the previous section. They are there because the word "flower" is part of their traditional name, although several look suspiciously like leaves.

Piecing some of the larger, leafy trees can be made much easier by using the new strip piecing techniques (see section 5). The books by Barbara Johnnah and Taimi Dudley listed in the Bibliography explain this method. Strip piecing is unorthodox, but works well when the block has many small square pieces. Don't let the many leaves of a very full tree stop you from proving America's favorite bad poet, Joyce Kilmer, partially wrong. "Only God can make a tree," but quilters can stitch a forest of them with the patterns in this chapter.

Diagonal Leafy Trees

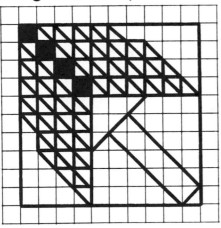
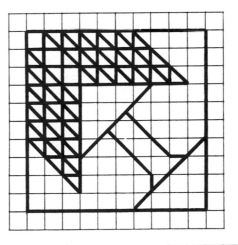
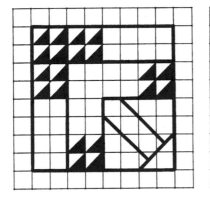
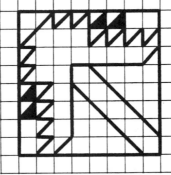
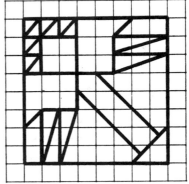
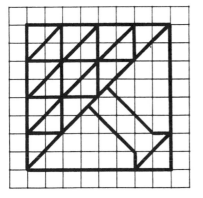

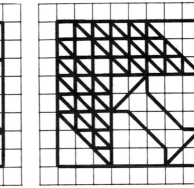
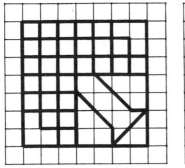
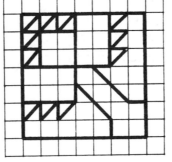
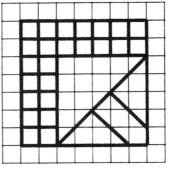

Diagonal Leafy Trees, CONTINUED

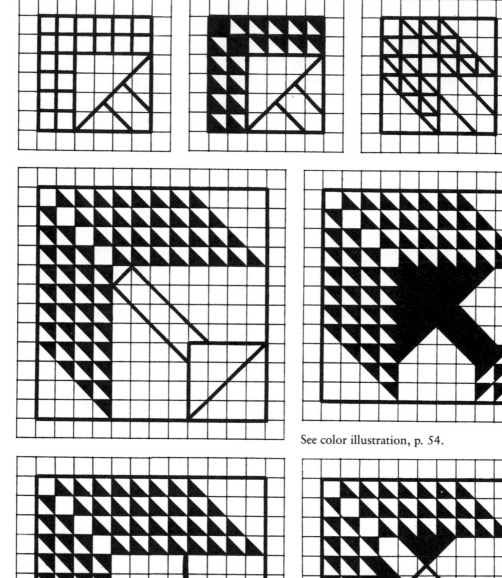

See color illustration, p. 54.

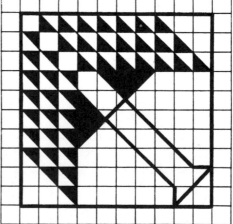

Diagonal Leafy Trees, CONTINUED

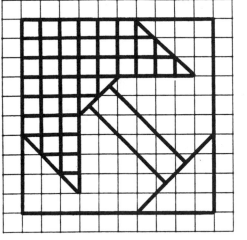
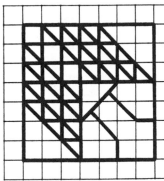
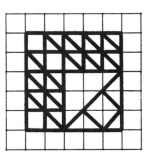

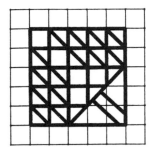
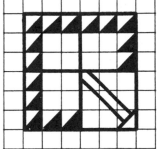
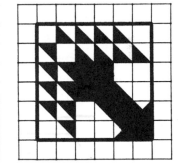

Leafy Trees on Diagonal Grids

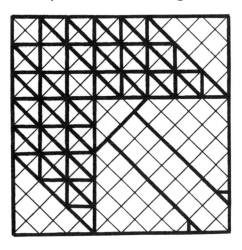

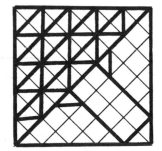

Diagonal Pine Trees

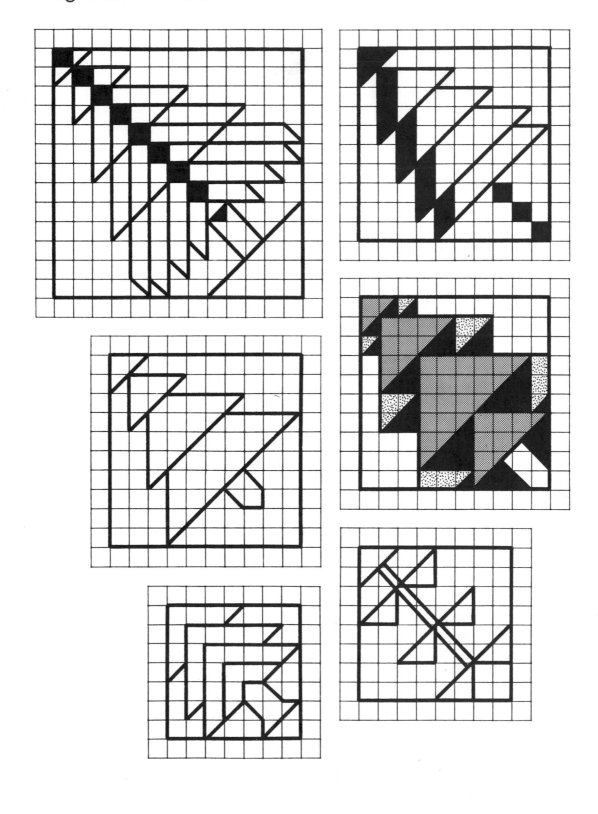

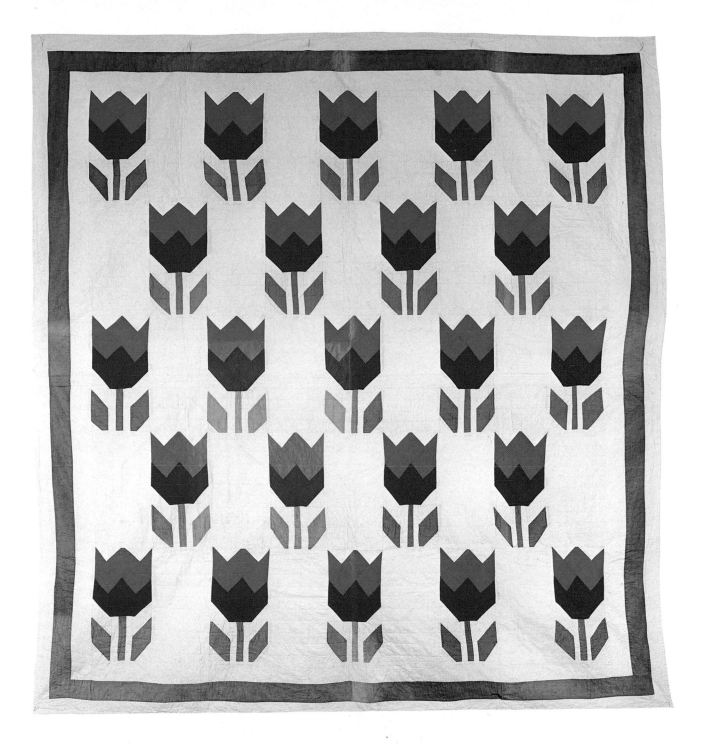

"Modernistic Tulips," Pennsylvania, c. 1910, cotton, 82″ x 76″. See p. 43 for pieced tulip design. Collection of Jonathan Holstein and Gail van der Hoof.

"Sweet Gum Leaf," by Pauline Magee, Harrisville, Mississippi, 1974, cotton, 85″ x 74½″. See p. 67 for pieced leaf design. Collection of State Historical Museum, Mississippi Department of Archives and History.

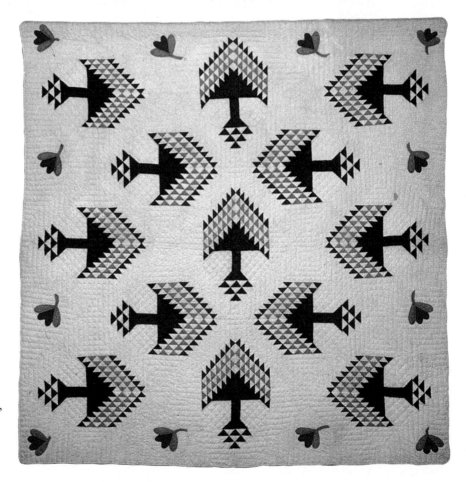

"Trees of Paradise," Indiana, c. 1840, cotton, 84″ square. See p. 50 for pieced tree design. Collection of Rosie Grinsted.

"Christmas Trees," Ohio, c. 1880, cotton, 80″ square. See p. 62 for pieced flowering-tree design. Courtesy of Mrs. Anne Cox. Photo by Roy L. Hale shown with permission of Leman Publications, Inc., Wheatridge, Colorado.

"Triangle Trees," Connecticut, c. 1865, cotton 83″ x 80″. See p. 58 for pieced repeating tree design. Collection of Judith and James Milne.

Upright Leafy Trees

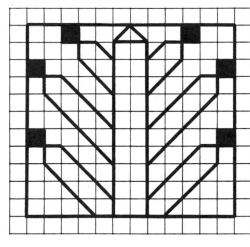

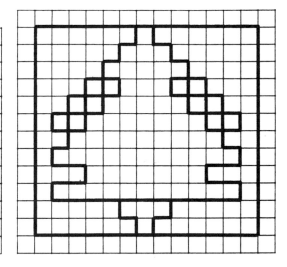

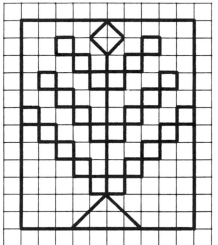

See color illustration, p. 35.

See color illustration, p. 35.

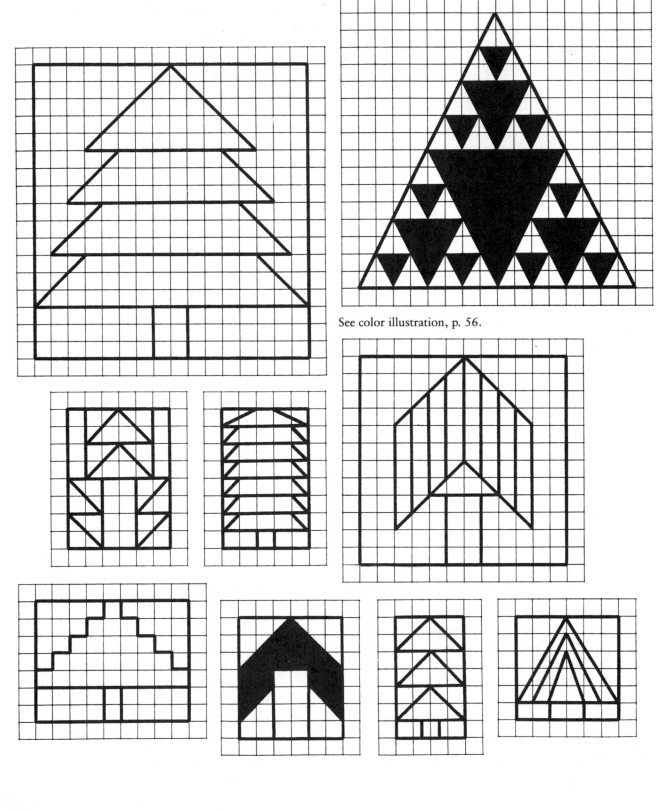

See color illustration, p. 56.

Upright Pine Trees, CONTINUED

 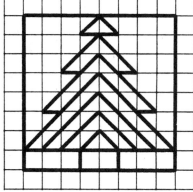 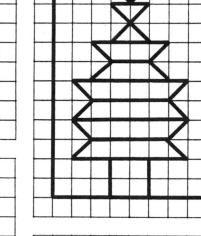

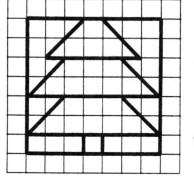 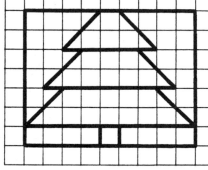 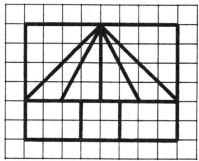

Pine Forests

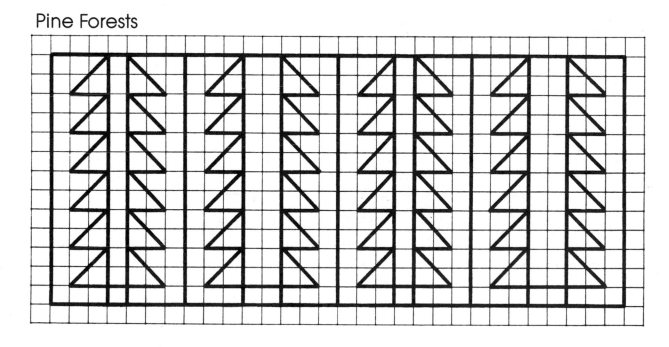

Pine Forests, CONTINUED

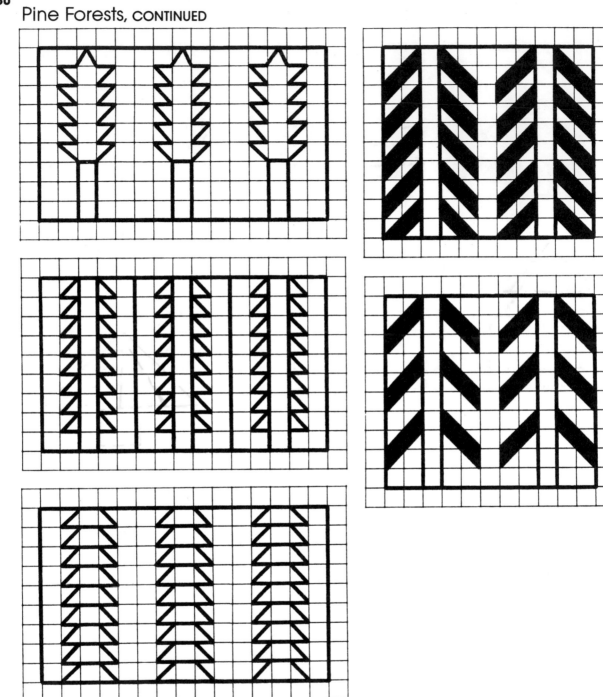

Christmas Trees

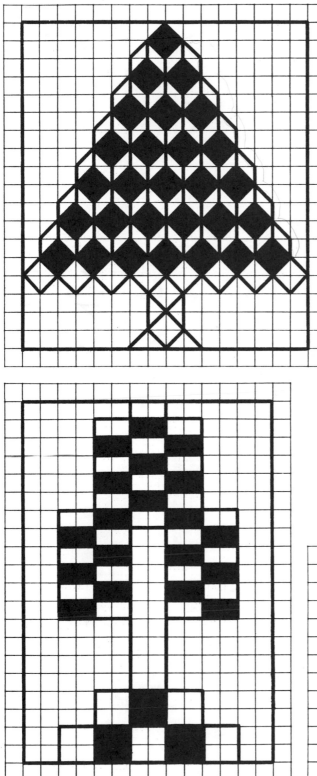

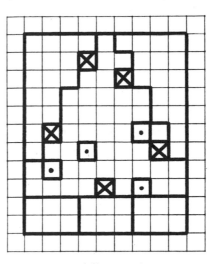

Ornaments in different colors.

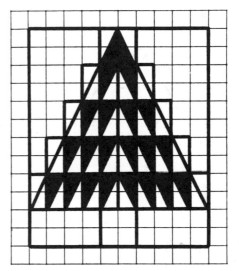

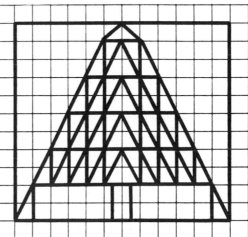

Flowering Trees

See color illustration, p. 55.

Apple and Cherry Trees

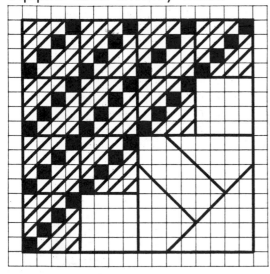

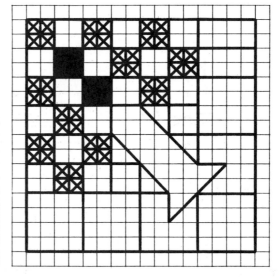

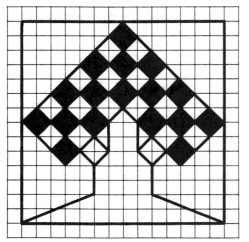

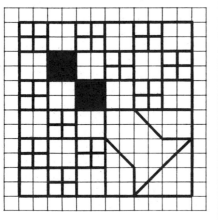

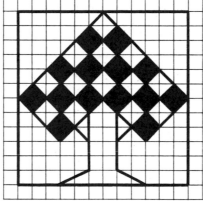

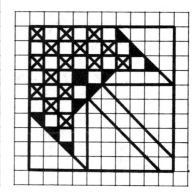

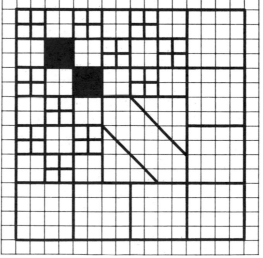

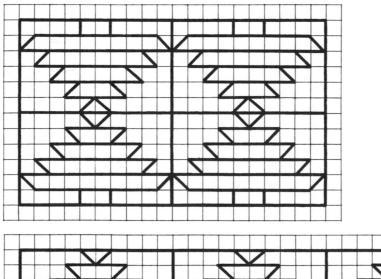

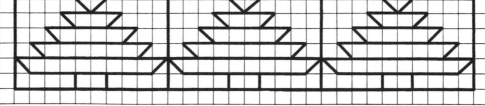

Tree Patterns from Woven Coverlets

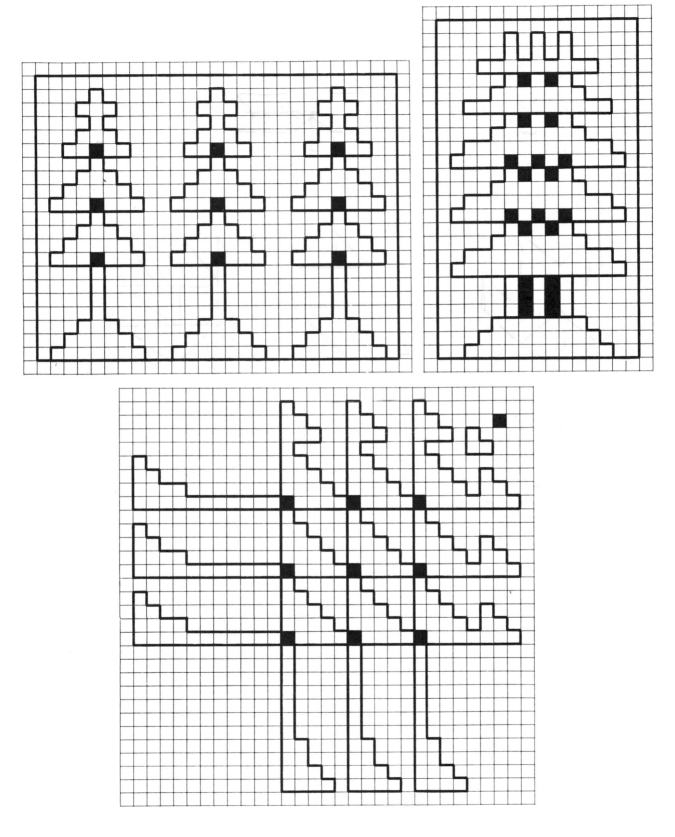

Leaves

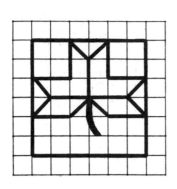

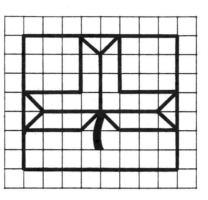

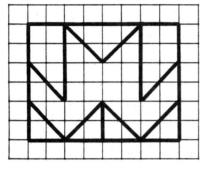

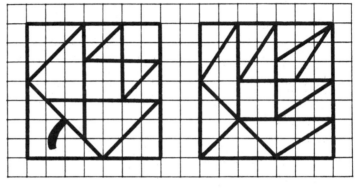

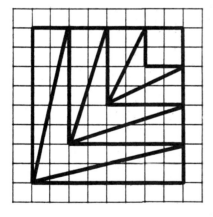

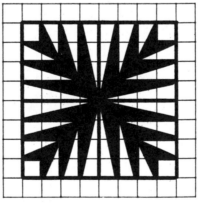

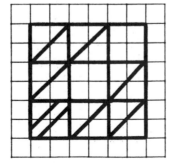

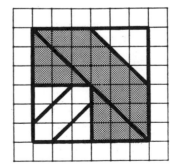

Leaves, CONTINUED

See color illustration, p. 54.

 4. Baskets

THE AMISH used basket patterns in many spectacular quilts that are as modern as a neon sign. It is the only representational pattern the "plain people" used regularly, apparently overcoming their usual reluctance to make images. Was the basket considered so humble and so useful that their fears of idolatry were dispelled?

The Amish used startling two- and three-color schemes, avoiding the white backgrounds that the rest of rural America seemed to prefer. Non-Amish basket quilts are often one color, red or blue against white, or scrap quilts. The latter have a homespun appeal to modern eyes. A very simple scrap basket, with an interesting setting, was used to commemorate all of America's quilts on a 13¢ postage stamp issued in March of 1978.

Contemporary quilters seem to ignore the charms of basket making in fabric. New ones are seldom seen in shows or published in magazines. Is it because the modern basket is usually made of plastic or paper and of no great beauty? Or does carrying things not have the significance in a motorized electronic society that it did in the small-town life of the nineteenth century?

Too bad, because the basket is one of the most versatile of patterns waiting to be rediscovered. A modern quilt can have a large single basket, many small ones, or different kinds of baskets to suggest the great variety available. Empty baskets are more formal, filled ones richer and more cheerful. Try tilting the baskets on their sides, having their contents spill out. Many of the baskets in this section will combine with the pieced flower patterns in section 2, and all but a few will accept appliquéd additions. Broderie perse, cutting images from printed fabric and appliquéing them in new arrangements, is perfect for filling baskets. Many contemporary textiles have traditional motifs of flowers or fruit which can be stitched into a basket. Or fill the basket with objects that aren't so obvious, ones that are silly or surreal or personal. Baskets were created to carry anything and everything.

The organization of this section differs slightly from the others in this book. There are so many possible basket variations that a drawing of each would fill the entire book. Instead, the three component parts of most baskets—base, body, and handle—are drawn separately in the opening pages. The three parts also include diagonal and upright versions. The would-be basket maker can combine almost any base with any body and handle, provided she sticks to either all diagonal or all upright forms. There are in all a possible 3,000 diagonal baskets and 1,377 upright ones. Have fun deciding—there's lots to choose from. A few of the most common combinations are given on the page labeled "5 x 5" (this means the block is five units square).

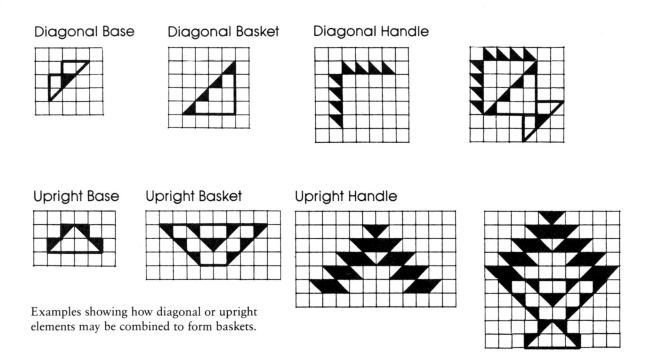

Diagonal Base Diagonal Basket Diagonal Handle

Upright Base Upright Basket Upright Handle

Examples showing how diagonal or upright
elements may be combined to form baskets.

The pages following, labeled "6 x 6," "7 x 7", etc., show more variations on the basic theme. Some have pieced flowers, some have quite different component parts, others suggest different settings. Look at them all. Try out the ones that are especially appealing. Experiment with some possible combinations. Make some bountiful baskets.

Diagonal Bases A

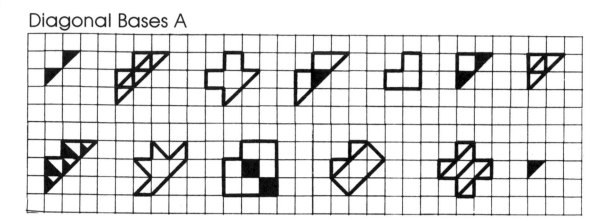

Diagonal Baskets A

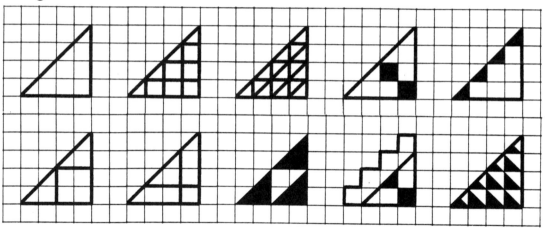

Diagonal Bases B

Diagonal Baskets B

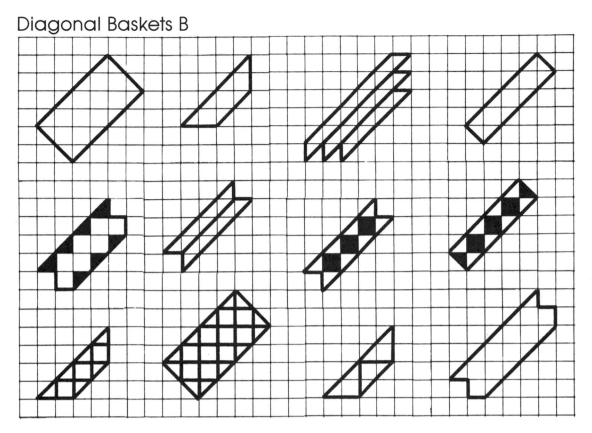

Diagonal Handles

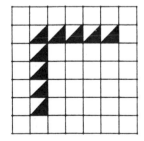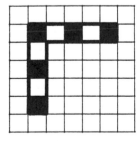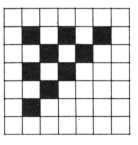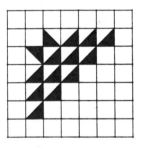

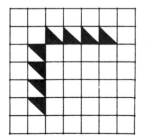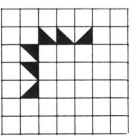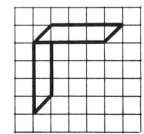

Upright Bases

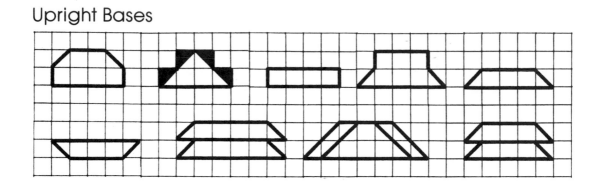

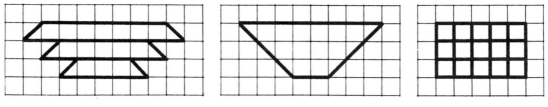

Upright Baskets

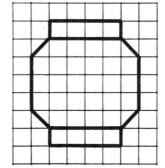

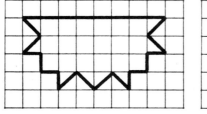

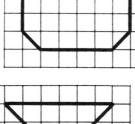

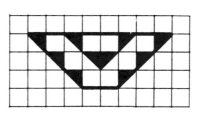

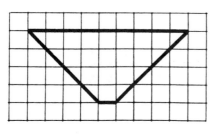

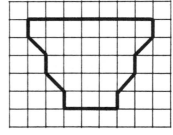

Upright Baskets, CONTINUED

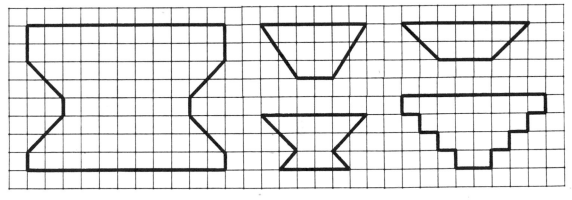

Upright Handles

5 x 5 Grid Baskets

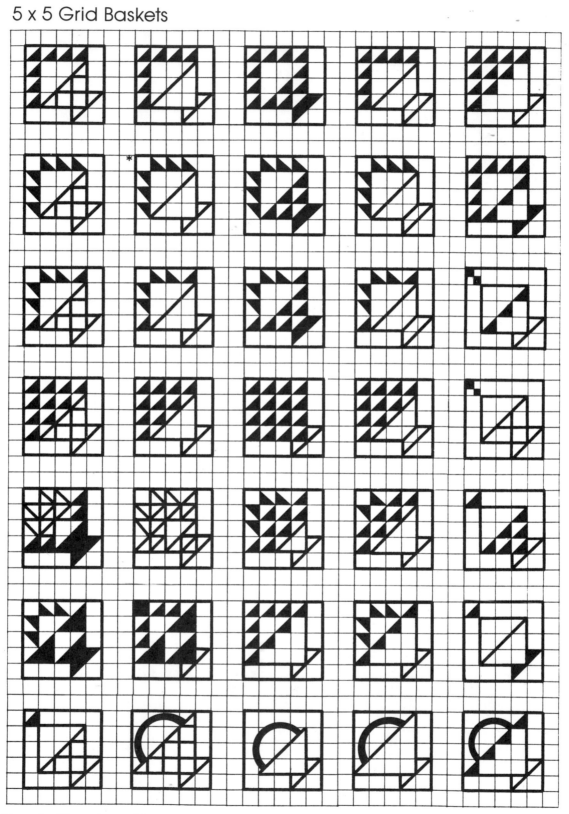

*See color illustration, p. 89.

6 x 6 Grid Baskets

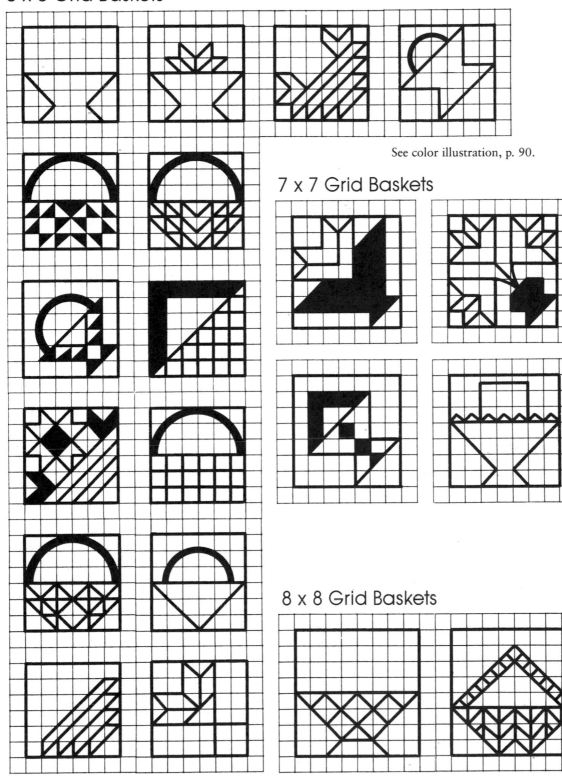

See color illustration, p. 90.

7 x 7 Grid Baskets

8 x 8 Grid Baskets

8 x 8 Grid Baskets, CONTINUED

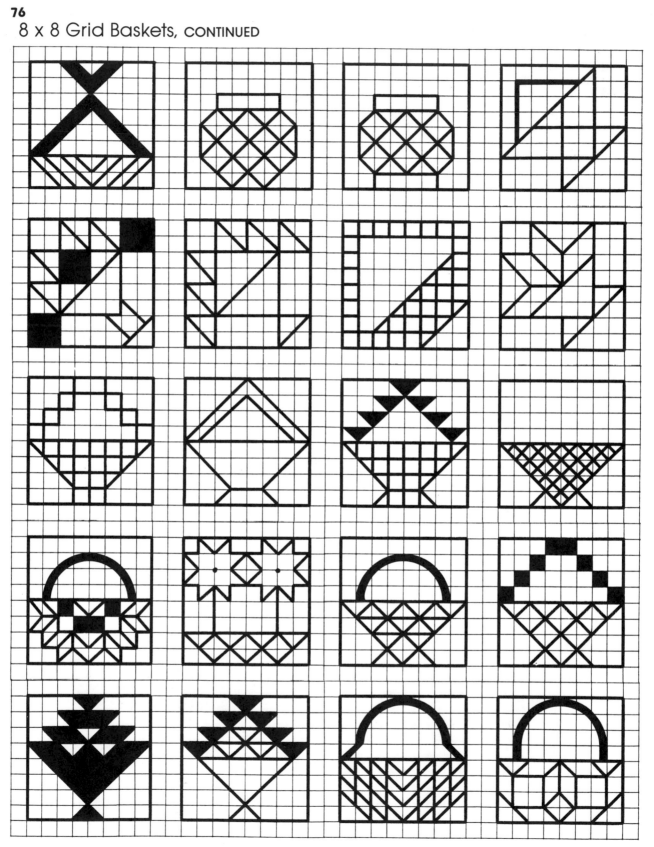

8 x 8 Grid Baskets, CONTINUED

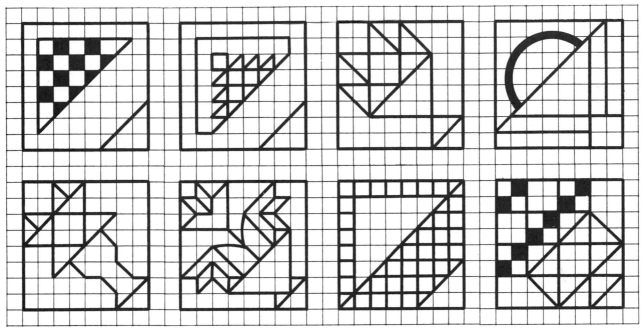

9 x 9 Grid Baskets

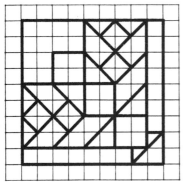
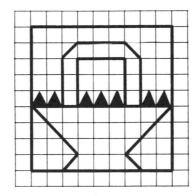
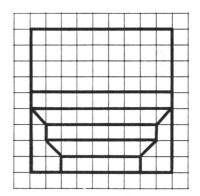

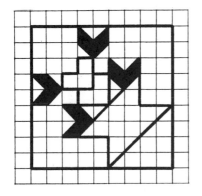
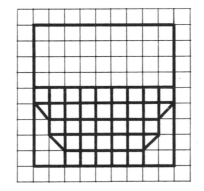
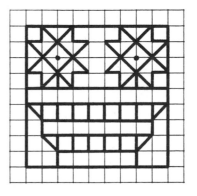

9 x 9 Grid Baskets, CONTINUED

10 x 10 Grid Baskets

12 x 12 Grid Baskets

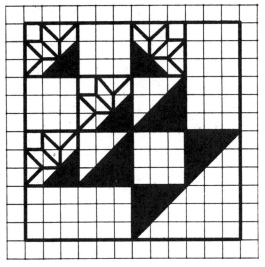

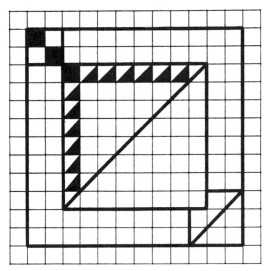

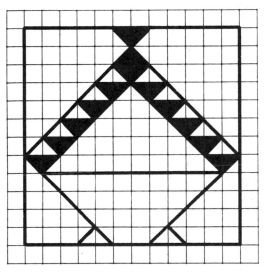

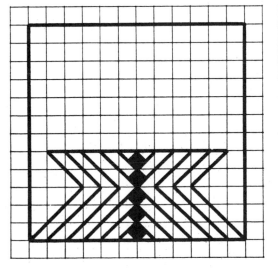

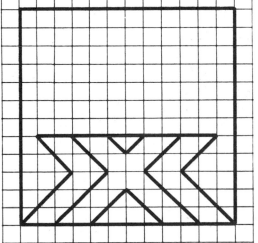

Rectangular Baskets

Quilt Stamp Block

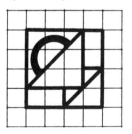

Quilt Stamp Block Setting

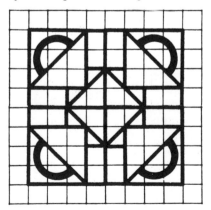

5. Alphabets and Messages

ALPHABET quilts were common in the nineteenth century. Some were like samplers, with the maker's name and date pieced very large. Others were clearly a mother's way of teaching her children their ABC's and 1, 2, 3's. The most ambitious had messages, usually from Scripture. The person who slept under one of these pious quilts was literally covered and kept warm by the "Good Word."

But as patterns were collected and published in the twentieth century, alphabets for quilters were unaccountably left out. As quilters became increasingly dependent on published patterns, the tradition of alphabet quilts gradually faded.

However, the idea of using words in a twofold way, as both pattern and message, is too good to be forgotten. Decorative letters form a pleasing pattern of their own, no matter what they spell out. And why shouldn't quilts, quite literally, speak to us?

Consider using a favorite saying or line of poetry or sweet endearment as a border. Pick one of the ornate alphabets, and its existence will be known only to a few. The casual observer will see only a linear or dotted pattern. Or do what early quilters did and piece the whole quilt as a message to the world, choosing the words that are meaningful to you.

Certain words go well with other kinds of patterns, such as "I Love You" and hearts, or "Holiday Greetings" and Christmas trees. Look in the other chapters for designs to illustrate your message. Or create an alphabet book quilt for a favorite child. A minimum of 52 blocks is needed, one for each letter of the alphabet and another one for a picture beginning with that letter. The following patterns are all contained in this book:

A = Arrow, Airplane
B = Butterfly, Boat, Bird, Bow, Basket, Bell
C = Cat, Cup, Cross, Chicken
D = Donkey, Dove, Dancer
E = Elephant, Eagle
F = Fish, Flag, Flower
G = Giraffe
H = Heart, Hat, House
I = Iris
J = Joy, Jack & Jill
K = Kite
L = Lantern, Ladder, Lily, Locomotive
M = Merry

N = Noel, Nine (number)
O = One (number)
P = Poppy, Pansy, Package
Q = Quilt
R = Rose, Rocking Horse
S = Sewing Machine, Sheep, Spool, Stocking
T = Train, Tree, Tulip
U = Umbrella
V = Vase
W = Windmill
X = Xmas Tree
Y = Yellow (square)
Z = Zero (number), Zebra (Donkey pieced in black and white stripes)

The alphabets in this chapter vary in size and complexity. The Fancy Alphabet will create a dotted pattern, no matter what you choose to say with it. The Sans Serif is the easiest and the smallest. The Thick and Thin is the most modern. The Block Letters the most formal. The Serif somewhat eccentric, but with a bold, strong pattern. Choose an alphabet that suits your message and whose design you like. Then graph the entire saying or series of words on graph paper before making the templates. This will ensure that the spacing of the letters is even and also indicate how much space the message will take up.

To piece the individual letters, use the strip piecing technique that has become so popular recently. It is an easy, but unorthodox, method. You sew long pieces of fabric together to make horizontal strips and then cut them vertically into ready-made blocks. To demonstrate the technique, the single letter "A" from the Fancy Alphabet shown on p. 95 has been plotted out.

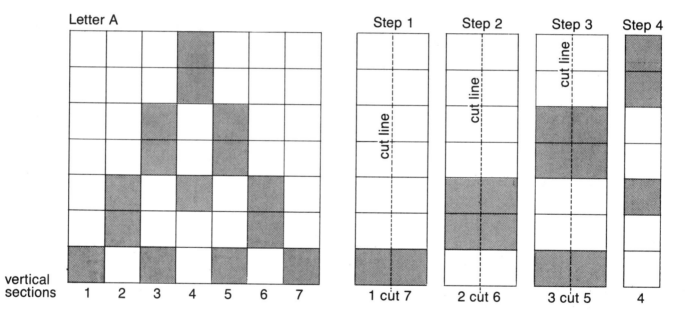

Letter A is 7 grid units high and 7 grid units wide. Step by step, here is how to proceed to make up the letter:

1. Sew one piece of background color 6 units high by 2 units wide to one strip of letter color 1 unit high by 2 units wide. These are then cut vertically to create sections 1 and 7 as noted above.

2. Sew three strips together, the first a background color piece 4 units high by 2 units wide; the second a letter color piece 2 units high by 2 units wide: and a third strip, a background color piece 1 unit high by 2 units wide. This joined piece is then cut vertically for sections 2 and 6.

3. Four horizontal strips must now be joined. These are, from top to bottom, a background color strip 2 units high by 2 units wide; a letter color strip 2 units high by 2 units wide; a background color strip 2 units high by 2 units wide; and a letter color strip 1 unit high by 2 units wide. After joining these strips, cut the piece vertically for sections 3 and 5.

4. You are now left only with creating a vertical section of four pieces made up, from top to bottom, of a letter color strip 2 units high by 1 unit wide; a second of the same dimension in background color; a letter color strip 1 unit high by 1 unit wide; and, last, a background color strip 2 units high by 1 unit wide.

To take full advantage of this time-saving technique when composing phrases or words, plot out all the letters you will need in terms of the number of identical vertical sections. Your horizontal strips will then be made long enough to suffice for the required number of vertical sections.

For more information about strip piecing, see the books by Taimi Dudley and Barbara Johnnah in the Bibliography. Even whole alphabets that look like they would be tedious to piece (the Fancy one, for instance) go much more quickly when strip pieced.

Revive an old tradition and create a quilt that speaks uniquely for you—a pieced alphabet or sampler quilt.

Block Alphabet

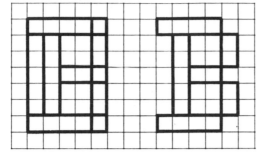

In order to make them readable, the alphabet letters are drawn as complete units and not as piecing blocks. The two letters at left show a complete "B" and a "B" divided into piecing blocks. The quilter can easily determine where piecing breaks should occur by studying the grid pattern of each letter.

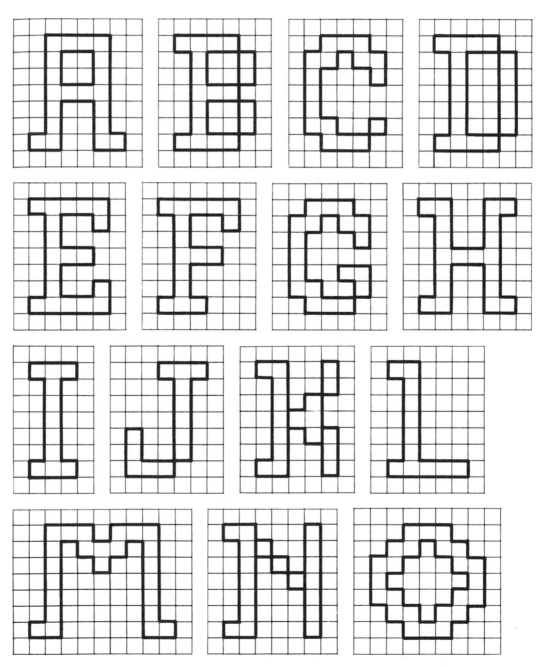

Block Alphabet, CONTINUED

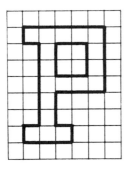
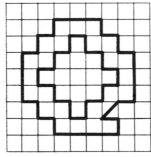
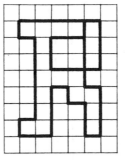

Sans Serif Alphabet

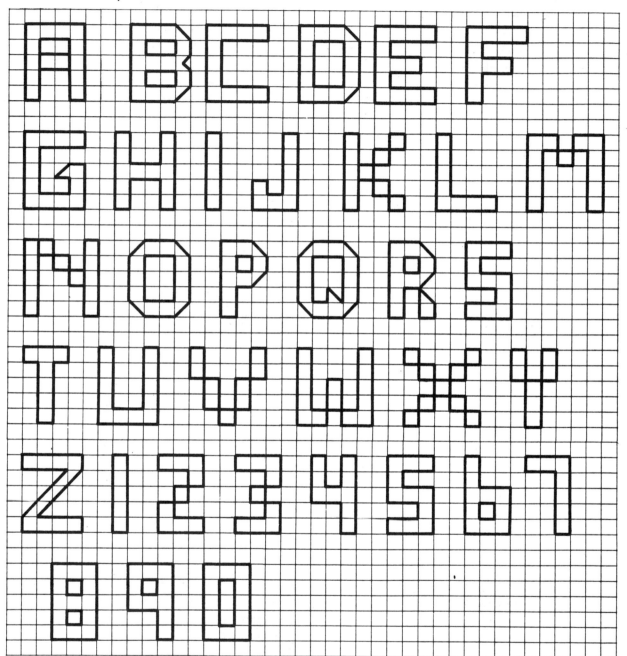

Thick and Thin Alphabet

Thick and Thin Alphabet, CONTINUED

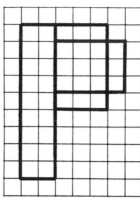

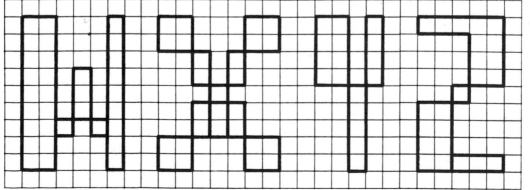

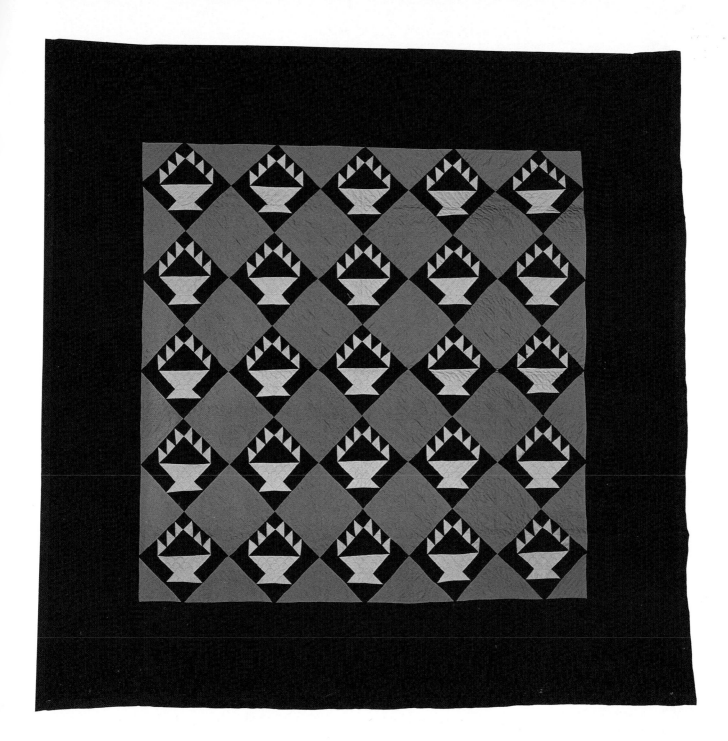

"Baskets," Pennsylvania, c. 1910, wool, 84″ square. See p. 74 for repeating pieced basket pattern. Collection of Phyllis Haders.

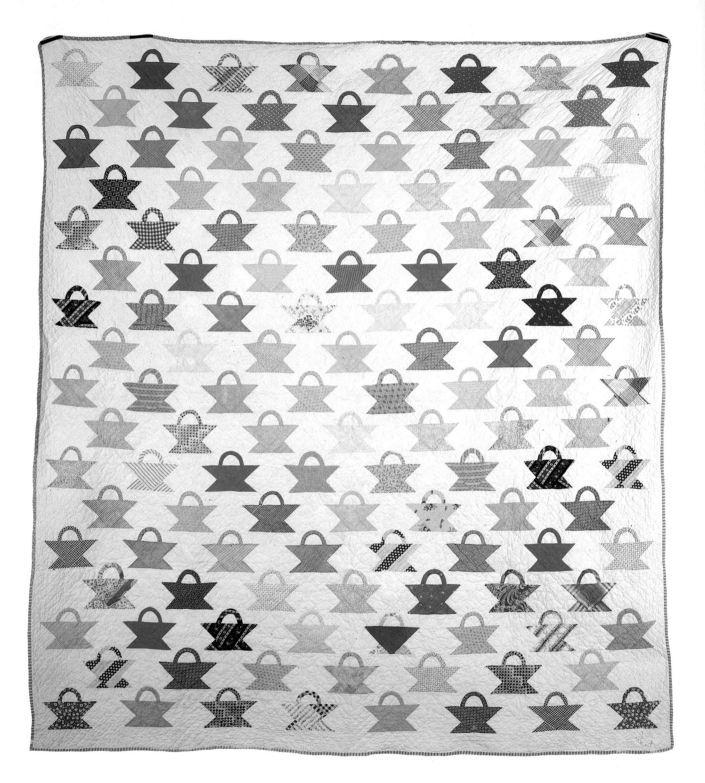

"Baskets," New York, c. 1865, cotton, 89″ x 80″. See p. 75 for piecing pattern. Collection of Judith and James Milne.

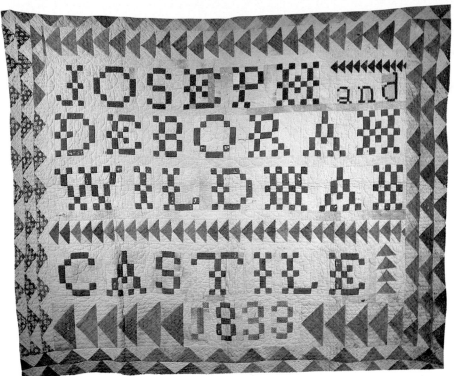

"The Wildman Quilt," Castille, New York, 1833, cotton, 80″ x 72″. Made for the marriage of Joseph and Deborah Wildman. See p. 95 for the pieced alphabet based on this quilt. New York State Historical Association, Cooperstown.

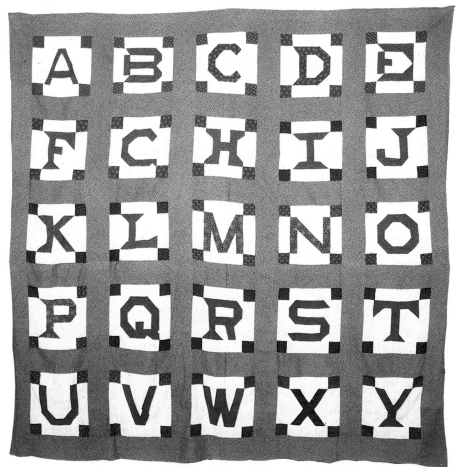

"Alphabet," Pennsylvania, c. 1890, cotton, 88″ x 82″. See p. 94 for a similarly pieced alphabet. Collection of Kelter-Malcé Antiques, New York City.

"Alphabet," Berks County, Pennsylvania, c. 1875, cotton, 80″ square. See p. 94 for a similarly pieced alphabet. Private collection.

Big Numbers

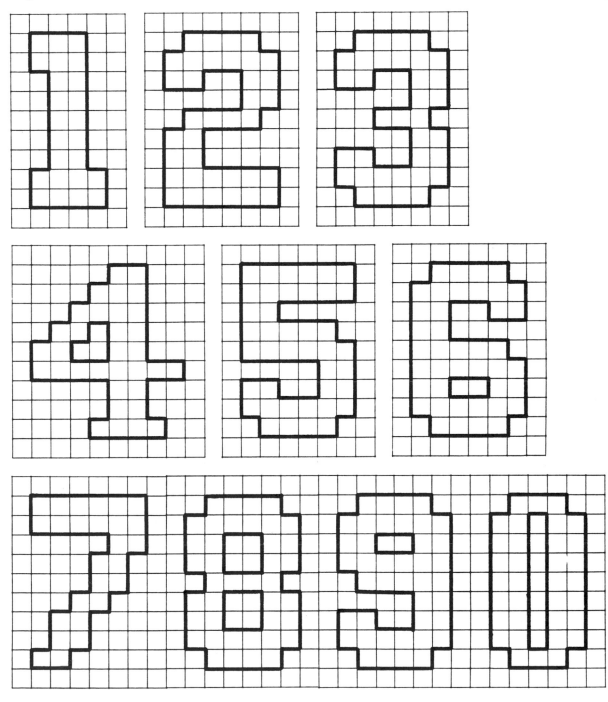

Serif Alphabet

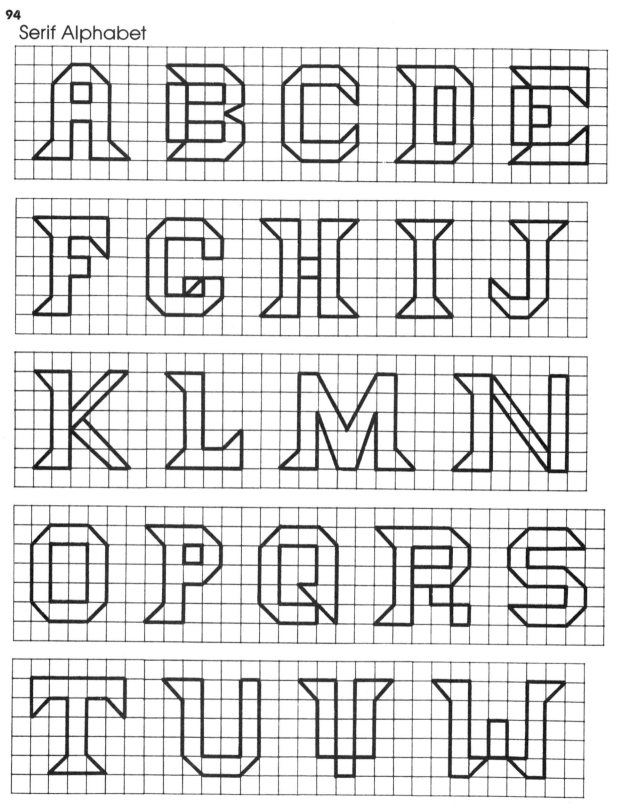

See color illustrations, pp. 91-92.

Serif Alphabet, CONTINUED

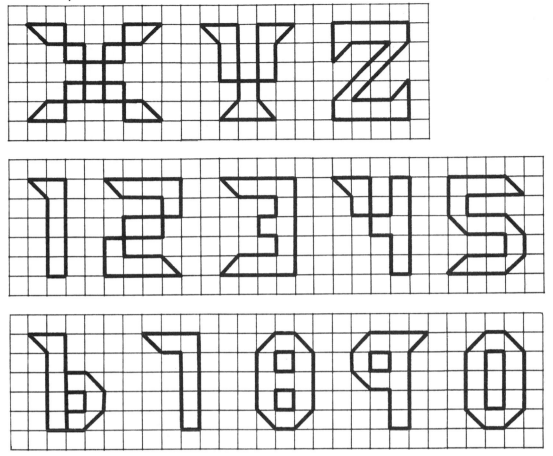

Fancy Alphabet

See color illustration, p. 91.

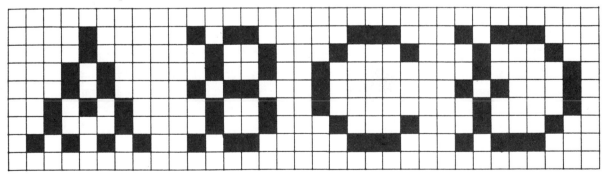

Fancy Alphabet, CONTINUED

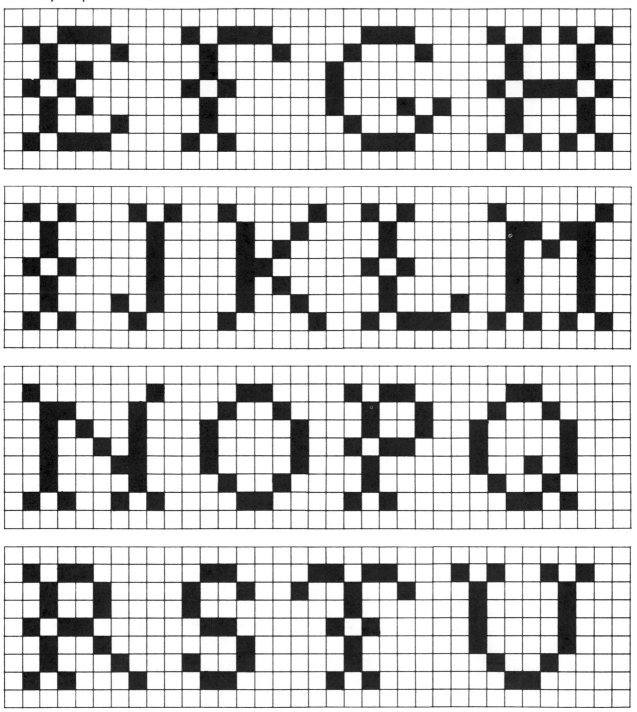

Fancy Alphabet, CONTINUED

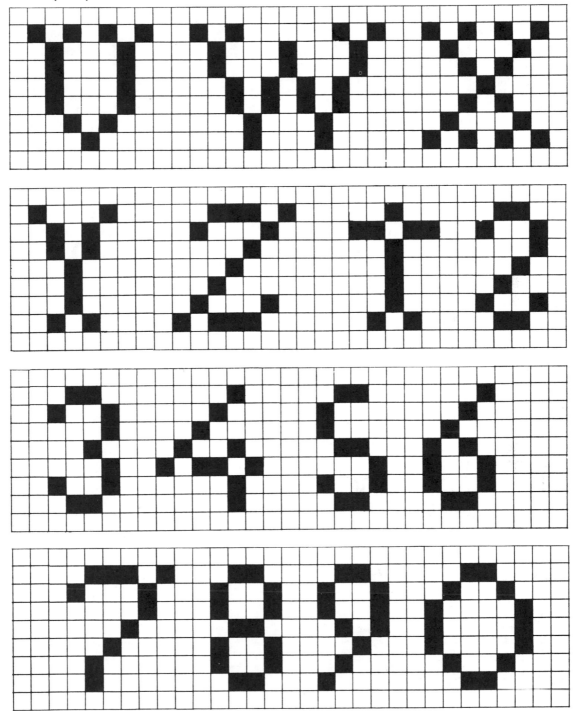

In building a message of connected letters, contrasting colors must be selected for each letter. When space is left between letters, the same color may be used.

6. People, Animals, and Objects

THIS section is very much like a Victorian attic. It contains all the leftovers, including lots of miscellaneous things a quilter might need—a sewing machine, a clown, a teddy bear.

Unlike most of the patchwork patterns in this book, these are largely twentieth-century creations. Birds and animals were abstract in early patterns (Wild Geese and Bear Paws), and designs depicting human beings were nonexistent. Bow ties were used before 1900, but as a simple pattern, not an article of clothing. Hearts were always appliquéd. The Centennial of 1876 occasioned lots of flag quilts, but they often incorporated printed flags instead of being pieced. Airplanes, trains, boats, tools, and household objects in general did not appear in fabric until this century.

Clearly, patchwork quilt design has not followed the same path as painting. Nineteenth-century quilts are boldly abstract, while the art of the time is totally representational. In the twentieth century art turns to the abstract while quilters begin to invent new pictorial patterns.

Quilting is a traditional craft, however, so even when real-life things are depicted, they are most often shown in a nonrealistic manner. Scenes, pictures, or stories are seldom stitched by quilters. Instead, an object (a coffeecup, for instance) or an image (a butterfly) is set in exactly the same way as the nonrepresentational patterns. The image is repeated over and over again, sometimes separated by a plain block, sometimes enclosed with sashing. Rare is the quilt that combines different images, sizes, or settings to create a thematic idea. Simple graphic repetition is the order of today as well as yesterday.

There is nothing wrong with this, of course. Repetition can create powerful design. However, a quilt depicting an air battle might be more appealing to a ten year old than airplanes lined up in a row. Broken hearts with flowers and zigzags of lightning tell an emotional story as well as a visual one.

The patterns in this section come from a wide variety of sources—some from quilts and coverlets, some invented, some from other crafts that rely on simple geometric patterns—needlepoint, cross-stitch, crocheting, and knitting. The quilter might be surprised to learn that there are few popular images that either have not, or cannot, be reduced to lines on graph paper. So, if you don't see what you want to piece in this chapter, look through other craft books, or buy some graph paper, and sharpen your pencil.

People

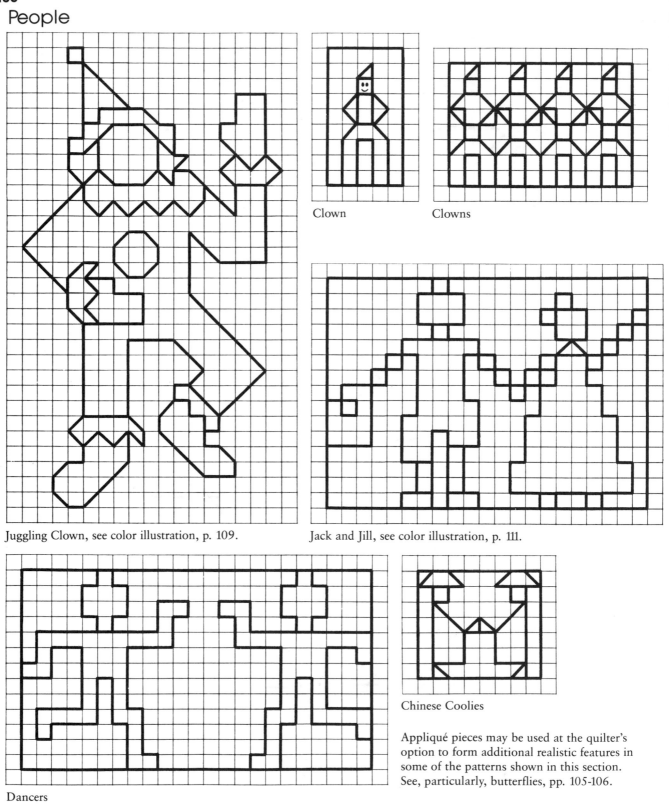

Clown

Clowns

Juggling Clown, see color illustration, p. 109.

Jack and Jill, see color illustration, p. 111.

Dancers

Chinese Coolies

Appliqué pieces may be used at the quilter's option to form additional realistic features in some of the patterns shown in this section. See, particularly, butterflies, pp. 105-106.

Animals

Elephant

Elephant

Donkey

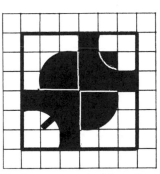

Turtle, composed of four Drunkard's Path patterns.

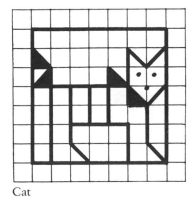

Cat

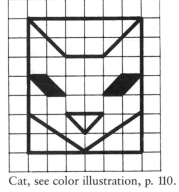

Cat, see color illustration, p. 110.

Animals, CONTINUED

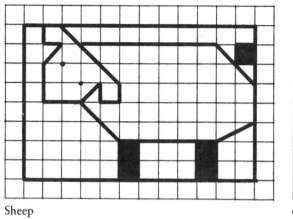

Sheep

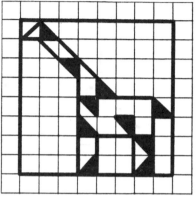

Giraffe

Toy Animals

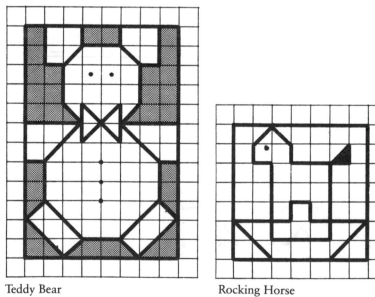

Teddy Bear

Rocking Horse

Birds

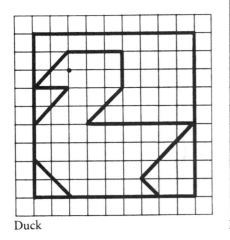

Duck

Rooster

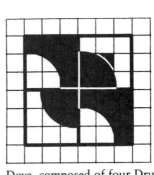

Dove, composed of four Drunkard's Path patterns.

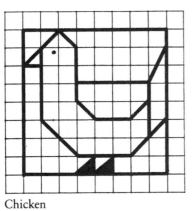

Chicken

Turkey

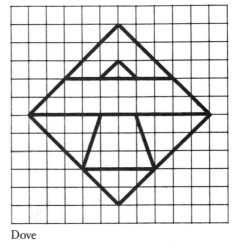

Dove

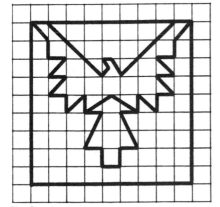

Eagle

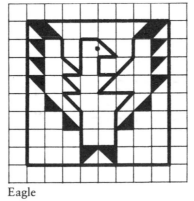

Eagle

Fishes

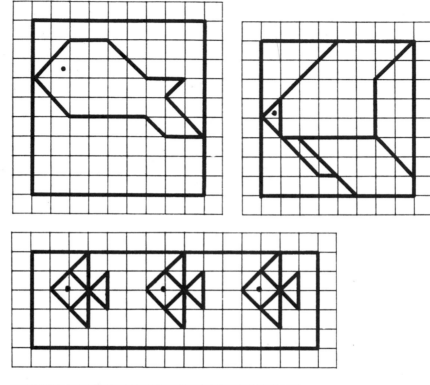

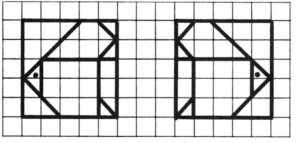

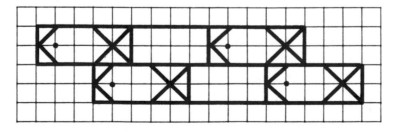

Butterflies

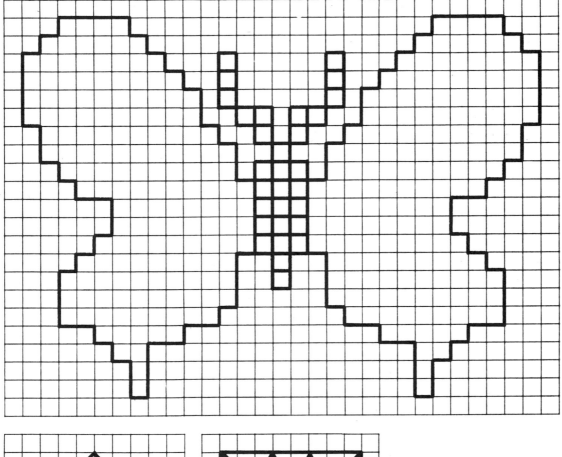

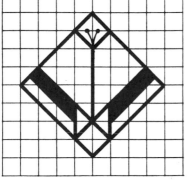

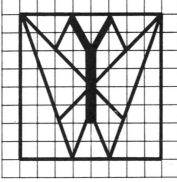

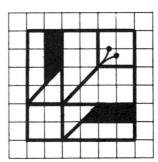

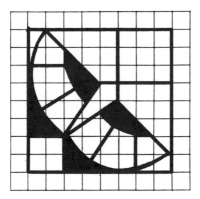

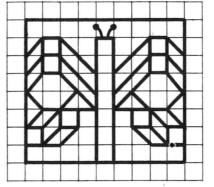

Butterflies, CONTINUED

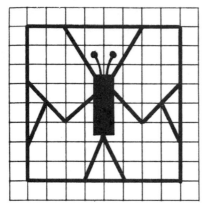
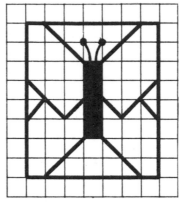
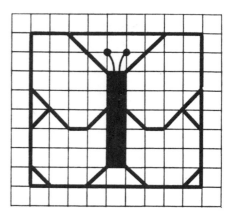

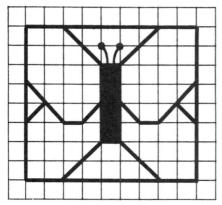
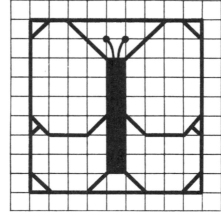
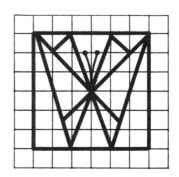

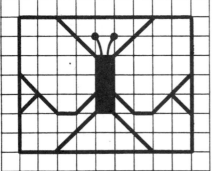
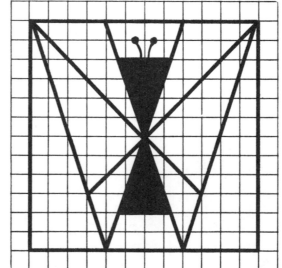

Trains

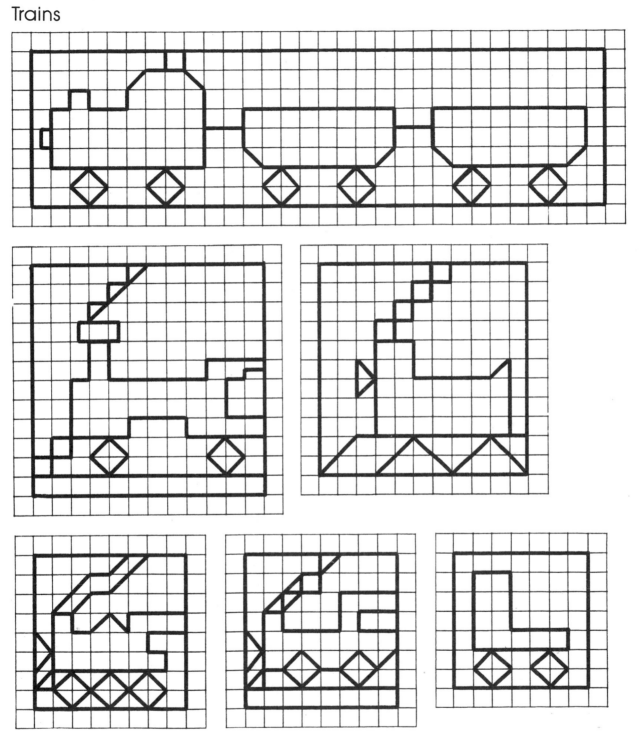

See also Train Stations, p. 29.

Boats

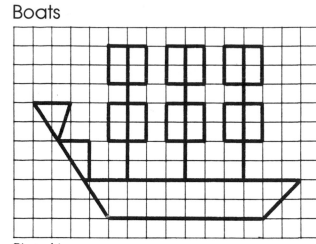

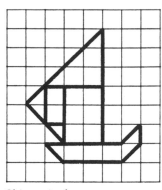

Pirate ship

Chinese junk

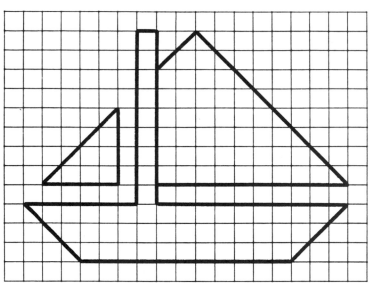

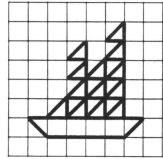

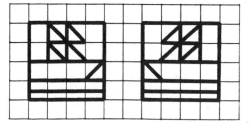

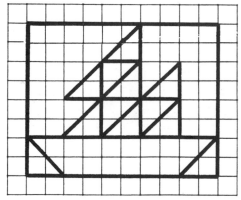

"Juggling Clown," by Jean Johnson, Anaheim, California, 1980, cotton-polyester blend, 90″ x 72″. See p. 100 for the pieced clown design. Courtesy of Jean Johnson; photo by Hazel Hynds.

"Cat Quilt," by Linda Platt, Chicago, Illinois. See p. 101 for pieced cat design. Courtesy of Linda Platt.

"Light in the Forest," by Jean V. Johnson, Maplewood, New Jersey, cotton, cotton blends, and silk, 1981, 44″ x 24″. Courtesy of Jean V. Johnson.

"Jack and Jill," by Ruth Ganeles, Columbia, Maryland, 1979, cotton and polyester, 84″ x 64″. See p. 100 for pieced pattern. Courtesy of Ruth Ganeles.

"Airplanes," by Thelma Faris, Lancaster, Kansas, c. 1939, cotton, 90″ x 78″. Made in memory of Kansas native Amelia Earhart. See p. 114 for repeating pieced airplane design. Courtesy of Thelma Faris.

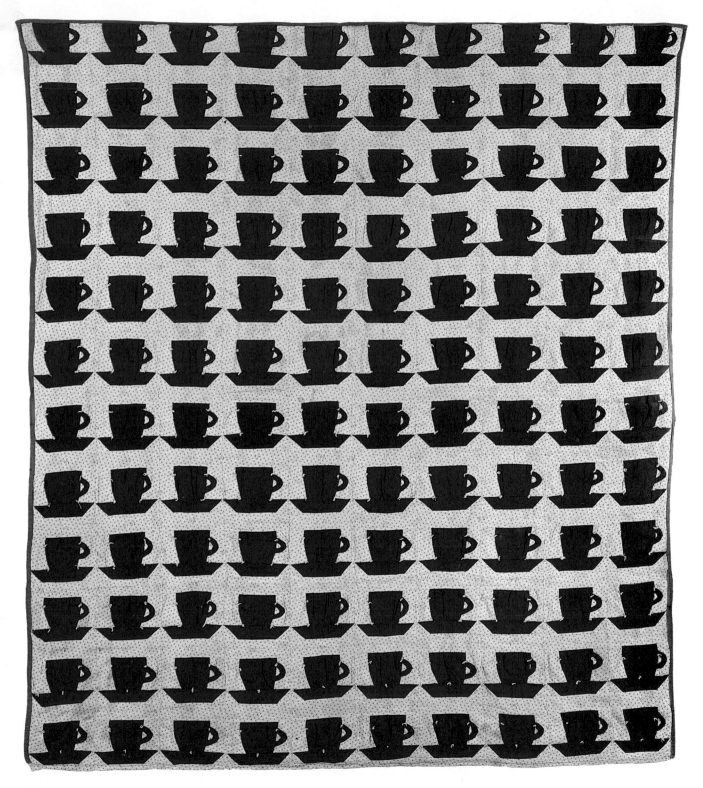

"Cup and Saucer," Colorado, c. 1910, cotton, 80½" x 69". See p. 122 for an interpretation of the cup and saucer pieced design. Collection of Jonathan Holstein and Gail van der Hoof.

Boats, CONTINUED

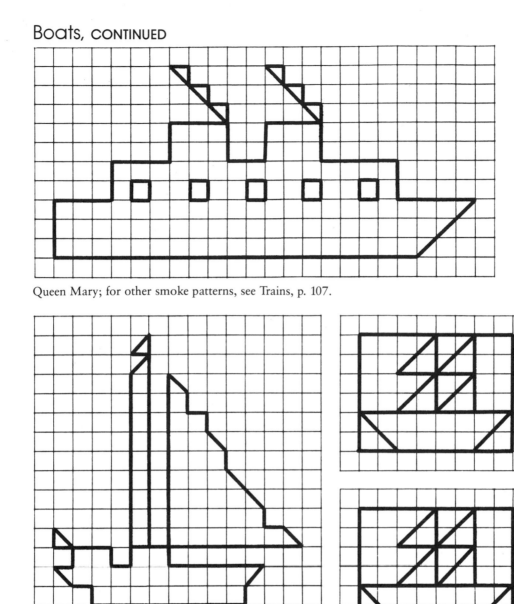

Queen Mary; for other smoke patterns, see Trains, p. 107.

Wave patterns, interchangeable

All boats can sail in the direction opposite that shown.

Airplanes

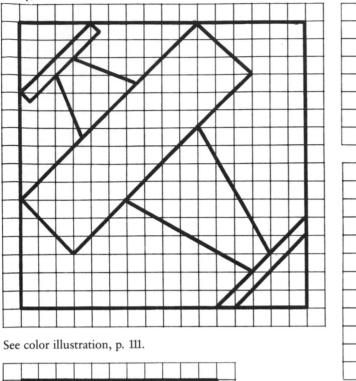

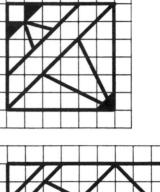

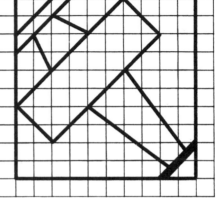

See color illustration, p. 111.

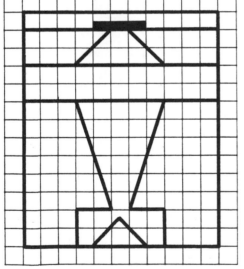

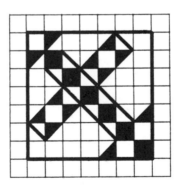

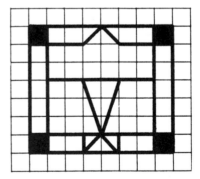

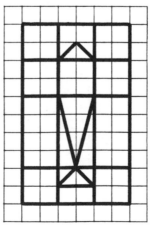

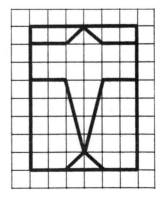

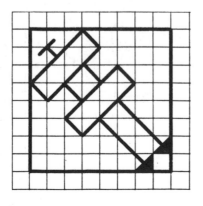

Airplanes, CONTINUED

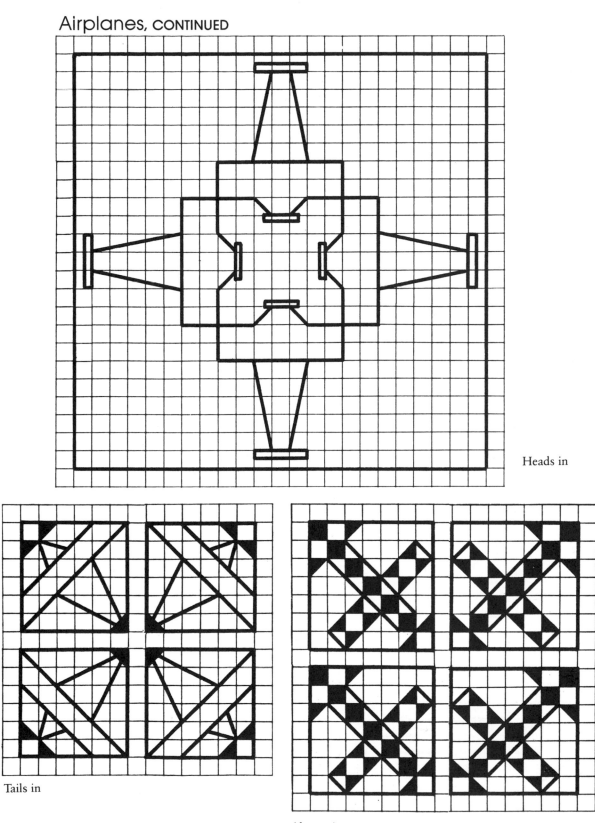

Heads in

Tails in

Alternative rows

Flags

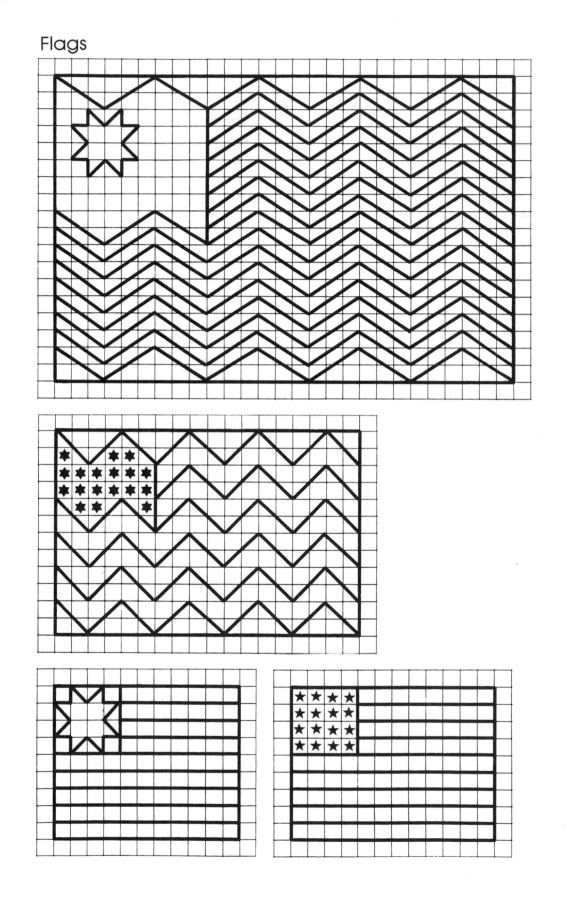

Ribbons and Bows

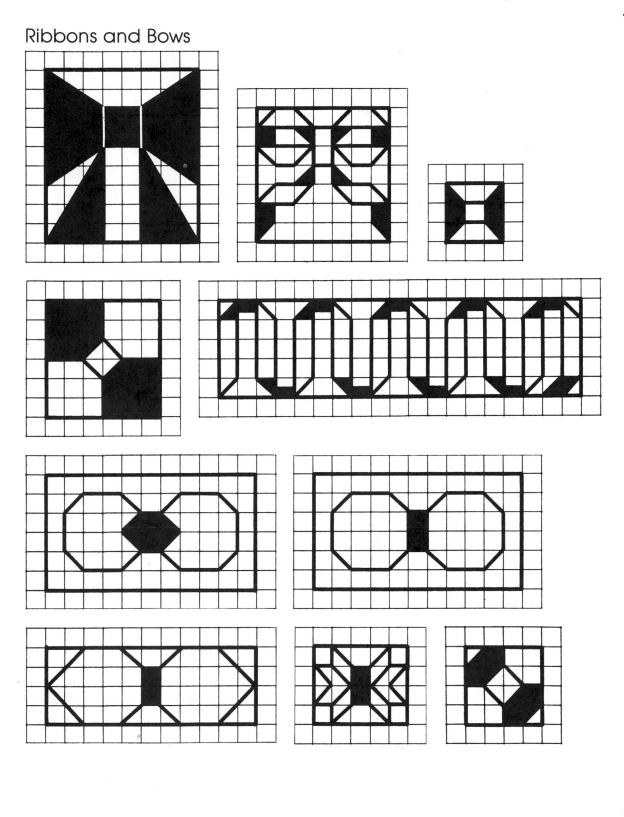

Hearts

Hearts, CONTINUED

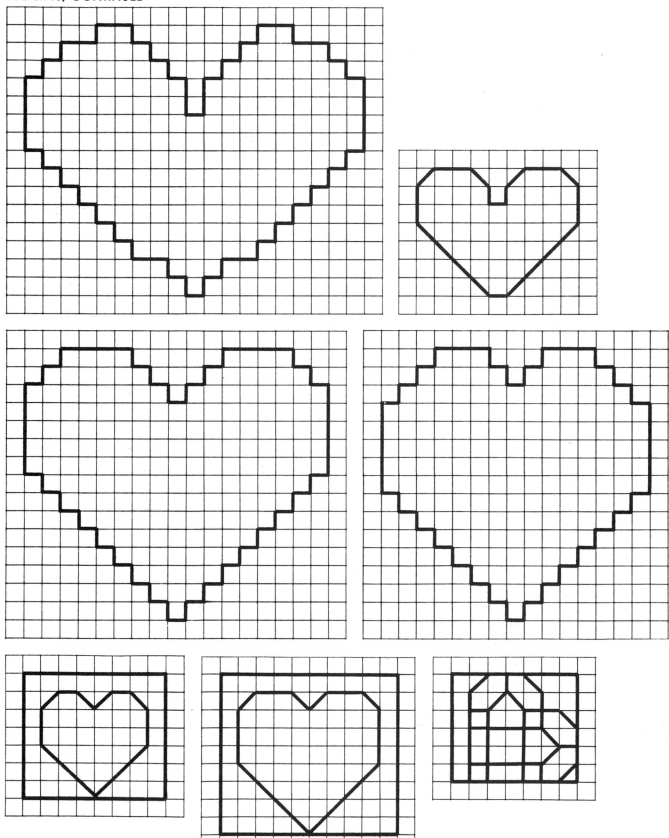

Hearts, CONTINUED

Broken Hearts   See Flowers, pp. 38-47; Arrows, p. 123; Messages, p. 98.

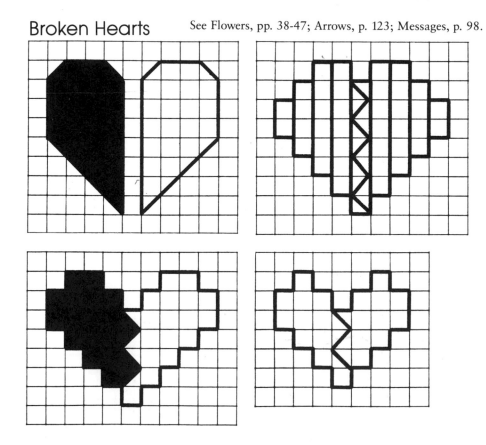

Broken Hearts, CONTINUED

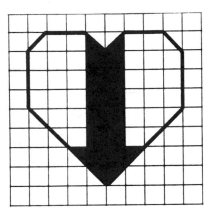

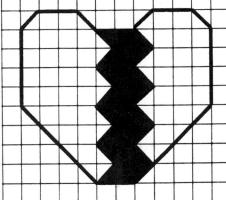

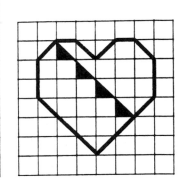

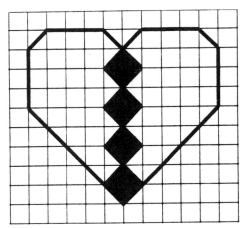

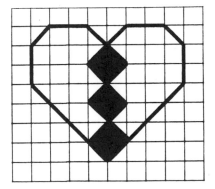

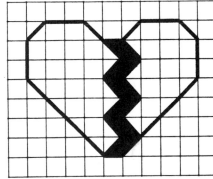

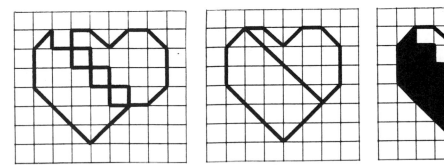

Miscellaneous

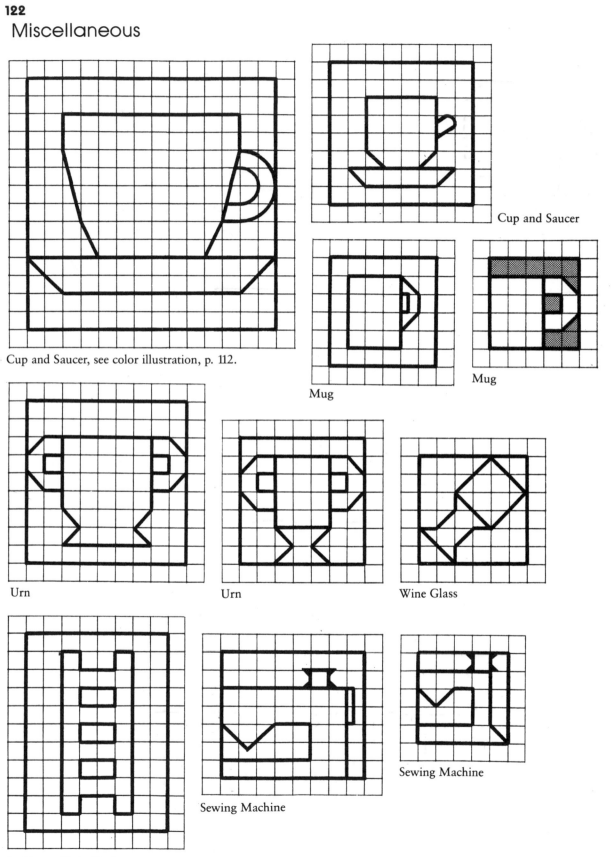

Cup and Saucer, see color illustration, p. 112.

Cup and Saucer

Mug

Mug

Urn

Urn

Wine Glass

Ladder or Train Track

Sewing Machine

Sewing Machine

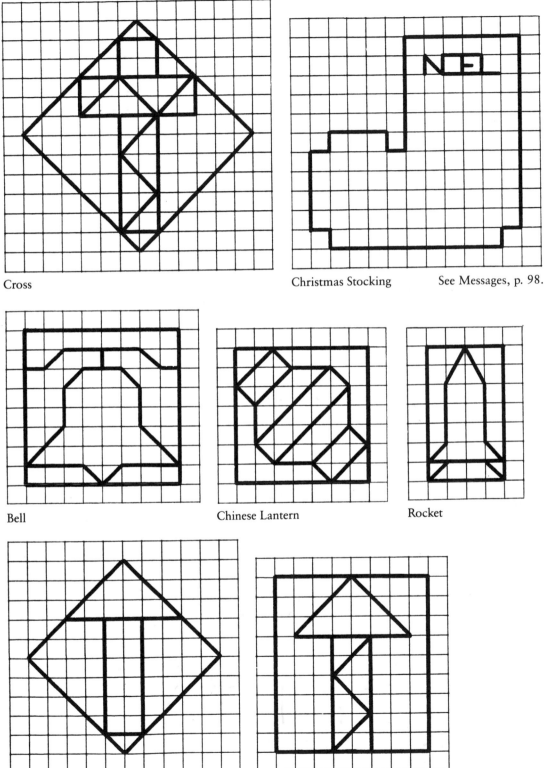

Miscellaneous, CONTINUED

Cross

Christmas Stocking   See Messages, p. 98.

Bell

Chinese Lantern

Rocket

Arrow

Arrow

Miscellaneous, CONTINUED

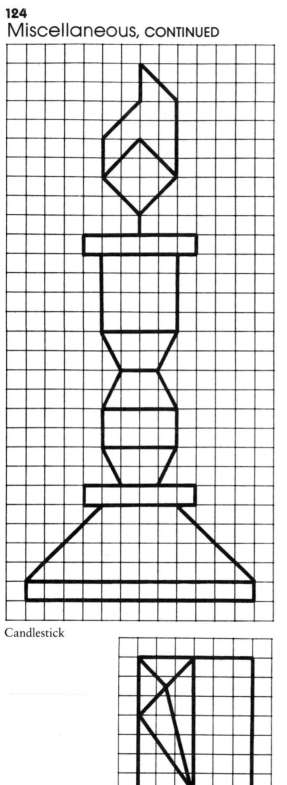

Candlestick

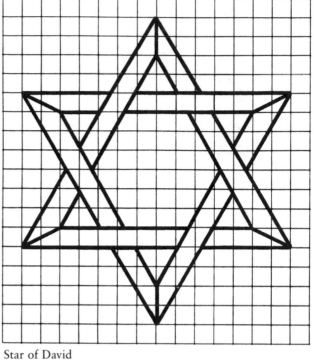

Star of David

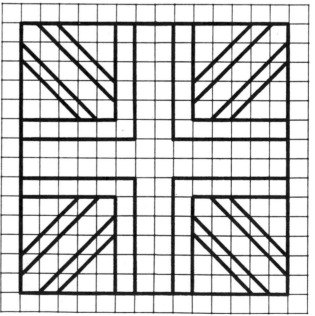

Union Jack

Kite

Bibliography

Albacete, M.J., Sharon D'Atri and Jane Reeves. *Ohio Quilts: A Living Tradition.* Canton, Ohio: The Canton Art Institute, 1981.

American Pieced Quilts. Washington: Smithsonian Institution, 1972.

Bacon, Lenice Ingram. *American Patchwork Quilts.* New York: William Morrow & Co., 1973.

Betterton, Sheila. *Quilts and Coverlets from the American Museum in Britain.* Bath, 1978.

Bishop, Robert. *New Discoveries in American Quilts.* New York: E.P. Dutton, 1975.

_____. *Quilts, Coverlets, Rugs and Samplers.* New York: Alfred A. Knopf, 1982.

Brackman, Barbara. *An Encyclopedia of Pieced Quilt Patterns.* 8 vols. Lawrence, Kans., 1979-83.

Burbidge, Pauline. *Making Patchwork for Pleasure and Profit.* London: John Gifford Ltd., 1981.

Burnham, Dorothy K. *Pieced Quilts of Ontario.* Toronto: Royal Ontario Museum, 1975.

Carlisle, Lillian Baker. *Pieced Work and Appliqué Quilts at Shelburne Museum.* Shelburne, Vt.: The Shelburne Museum, 1957.

Chase, Pattie, with Mimi Dolbier. *The Contemporary Quilt: New American Quilts and Fabric Art.* New York: E.P. Dutton, 1978.

Colby, Averil. *Patchwork.* Newton Centre, Mass.: Charles T. Branford, 1958.

Conroy, Mary. *300 Years of Canada's Quilts.* Toronto: Griffin House, 1976.

Davison, Mildred. *American Quilts from the Art Institute of Chicago.* Chicago, 1966.

Dudley, Taimi. *Strip Patchwork.* New York: Van Nostrand Reinhold, 1980.

Finley, John and Jonathan Holstein. *Kentucky Quilts, 1800-1900.* Louisville: The Kentucky Quilt Project, Inc., 1982.

Finley, Ruth E. *Old Patchwork Quilts.* Newton Centre, Mass: Charles T. Branford, 1929.

Frye, L. Thomas. *American Quilts: A Handmade Legacy.* Oakland, Ca: The Oakland Museum, 1981.

The Great American Cover-up: Counterpanes of the Eighteenth and Nineteenth Centuries. Baltimore: Baltimore Museum of Art, 1971.

Gutcheon, Beth. *The Perfect Patchwork Primer.* New York: David McKay Company, Inc. 1973.

Haders, Phyllis. *The Main Street Pocket Guide to Quilts.* Pittstown, N.J.: The Main Street Press, 1983.

Holstein, Jonathan. *The Pieced Quilt: An American Design Tradition.* Greenwich, Conn.: The New York Graphic Society, Ltd., 1973.

Houston, Julie. *Woman's Day Prize-Winning Quilts, Coverlets and Afghans.* New York: Sedgewood Press, 1982.

Houck, Carter and Myron Miller. *American Quilts and How to Make Them.* New York: Charles Scribner's Sons, 1975.

Ickis, Marguerite. *The Standard Book of Quiltmaking and Collecting.* New York: Dover Publications, 1949.

Johnnah, Barbara. *Quick Quilting: Make A Quilt This Weekend.* New York: Drake Publishers, 1976.

Johnson, Bruce. *A Child's Comfort.* New York: Harcourt Brace Jovanovich, 1977.

Johnson, Mary Elizabeth. *Prize Country Quilts*. Birmingham, Ala.: Oxmoor House, 1977.

Khin, Yvonne M. *The Collector's Dictionary of Quilt Names and Patterns*. Washington: Acropolis Books, 1980.

Laury, Jean Ray. *Quilts and Coverlets: A Contemporary Approach*. New York: Van Nostrand Reinhold, 1970.

McKim, Ruby. *One Hundred and One Patchwork Patterns*. New York: Dover Publications, 1962.

Made By Hand: Mississippi Folk Art. Jackson: Mississippi State Historical Museum, 1980.

Malone, Maggie. *Classic American Patchwork Quilt Patterns*. New York: Sterling Publishing, 1980.

Mattera, Joanne. *The Quiltmaker's Art: Contemporary Quilts and Their Makers*. Asheville, N.C.: Lark Books, 1982.

Mills, Susan Winter. *Illustrated Index to Traditional American Quilts*. New York: Arco Publishing Co., 1980.

Museum of Contemporary Crafts. *The New American Quilt*. New York: American Crafts Council, 1976.

New Jersey Quilters: A Timeless Tradition. Morristown, N.J.: Morris Museum of Arts and Sciences, 1983.

North Carolina Country Quilts: Regional Variations. Chapel Hill, N.C.: Ackland Art Museum, n.d.

Olmstead, Janice. *A Dictionary of Patchwork Patterns*. Monrovia, Ca.: The Mail Pouch, 1976.

150 Years of American Quilts. Lawrence, Kans.: University of Kansas Museum of Art, 1973.

Orlofsky, Patsy and Myron Orlofsky. *Quilts in America*. New York: McGraw-Hill Book Co., 1974.

Patchwork: The Quilter's Guild Exhibit. London: Seven Dials Gallery, 1981.

Pforr, Effie Chalmers. *Award Winning Quilts*. Birmingham, Ala.: Oxmoor House, 1974.

Quilter's Choice: Quilts from the Museum Collection. Lawrence, Kans.: Helen Foresman Spencer Museum of Art, 1978.

Quilting Patchwork and Appliqué, 1700-1982: Sewing as a Woman's Art. London: Crafts Council Gallery, 1983.

Quilts and Carousels: Folk Art in the Firelands. A Sesquicentennial Exhibition. Oberlin, Ohio: Firelands Association for the Visual Arts, 1983.

Quilts and Counterpanes in the Newark Museum. Newark: Newark Museum, 1948.

Quilts and Coverlets. Denver: Denver Art Museum, 1974.

Quilts and Coverlets. Washington-on-the-Brazos, Tex.: Star of the Republic Museum, 1975.

Quilts from the Collection of the Oklahoma Historical Society. Tulsa: Oklahoma Historical Society, n.d.

Rehme, Judy. *Key to 1000 Quilt Patterns*. Richmond, Ind., 1978.

Safford, Carleton L. and Robert Bishop. *America's Quilts and Coverlets*. New York: E.P. Dutton, 1972.

Shogren, Linda. *The Quilt Pattern Index*. San Mateo, Ca.: Pieceful Pleasures, 1981.

Something to Keep You Warm: The Roland Freeman Collection of Black American Quilts from the Mississippi Heartland. Jackson: Mississippi State Historical Museum, 1981.

Southern Comfort: Quilts from the Atlanta Historical Society Collection. Atlanta: Atlanta Historical Society, 1978.

Vote, Marjean. *Patchwork Pleasure: A Pattern Identification Guide.* Des Moines: Wallace Homestead, 1960.

Wiss, Audrey and Douglas Wiss. *Folk Quilts and How to Recreate Them.* Pittstown, N.J.: The Main Street Press, 1983.

Woodward, Thomas K. and Blanche Greenstein. *Crib Quilts and Other Small Wonders.* New York: E.P. Dutton, 1981.